D1476821

NUMBER SIX

*Essays on the American West
sponsored by the
Elma Dill Russell Spencer Foundation*

Juan Davis Bradburn

Juan Davis Bradburn

A REAPPRAISAL OF THE MEXICAN

COMMANDER OF ANAHUAC

BY

Margaret Swett Henson

With the research assistance of
John V. Clay

TEXAS A&M UNIVERSITY PRESS

College Station

Library of Congress Cataloging in Publication Data

Henson, Margaret Swett, 1924–
    Juan Davis Bradburn: a reappraisal of the Mexican
commander at Anahuac.

    (Essays on the American West; no. 6)
    Bibliography: p.
    Includes index.
        1. Texas—History—To 1846.   2. Texas—History—
Revolution, 1835–1836—Causes.   3. Bradburn, Juan Davis,
1787–1842.   4. Soldiers—Mexico—Biography.   5. Soldiers
—United States—Biography.   I. Title.   II. Series.
F389.H48   1982   976.4   82-40312
ISBN 0-89096-135-2

Manufactured in the United States of America

FIRST EDITION

Contents

Acknowledgments

JOHN V. CLAY, a long-term resident of the Houston area whose avocation is history and archaeology, suggested this reassessment of Juan Davis Bradburn. For years Clay has been collecting source materials about Bradburn, and he generously provided me with copies from his files.

I am also indebted to Clay and Alan Probert, of Laguna Hills, California, for their translations of Bradburn's "Memorial" and other Spanish documents. With their permission the "Memorial" appears in Appendix 1 as a composite translation representing their efforts and mine.

MARGARET SWETT HENSON

Juan Davis Bradburn

The Legend

J UAN DAVIS BRADBURN, the Virginia-born commandant of the Mexican garrison at Anahuac in 1831 and
1832, remains one of the most maligned men in historical accounts of that period. Moreover, in 1832 he
dared to imprison William Barret Travis, a martyr at
the Alamo four years later, an act that allowed Texans
to remember Bradburn as an evil man who had to flee
when the settlers rebelled and seized the Mexican
forts at Velasco and Anahuac.

The first recorded criticism of Bradburn appears
in a letter of June, 1832, from Stephen F. Austin in
Matamoros to his associate Samuel May Williams.
Having received a "wild account" about trouble at
Anahuac, the empresario admitted that he had no details but supposed that Bradburn had acted hastily
and in passion. "The fact is he is incompetent to such
a command and is half crazy part of his time." At
about the same time John Austin, a distant cousin of
the empresario and commander of the force that captured Velasco, referred to Bradburn's "many despotic
and arbitrary acts" in his defensive report citing the

reasons for his attack on the government outpost on the Brazos River.[1]

Fortunately for the Texas rebels in 1832, their seizure of Velasco and Anahuac coincided with Federalist victories over Centralist posts near Matamoros. Thus the attack on Bradburn was viewed as a protest against the Centralist administration and a part of the civil war that had been continuing for several years. Bradburn, a supporter of the defeated Centralist faction, returned to the Rio Grande, where the war continued until Federalist Antonio López de Santa Anna managed to win the presidency. When Santa Anna invaded the recalcitrant state of Texas in 1836, Bradburn was again in the army. He failed to reach the centers of action and remained as commander of the port at Copano, but his enemies from 1832 spoke about him as though he had appeared in their midst.

The "wretch" presented his "accursed visage," coming as an "evil spirit, hovering, with gloomy and malignant aspect, in the rear of Santa Anna's army." These words appear in Henry Stuart Foote's *Texas and the Texans; or, Advance of the Anglo-Americans to the South-West*, published in 1841. Foote visited Texas in 1839 and interviewed, among others, Dr. Branch T. Archer, who had participated in Bradburn's defeat and was well known for his hyperbole. Whether the words are Archer's or Foote's matters little, because the sentiment expressed the popular view of Bradburn of the time. The colonel was sent to Texas to

[1] S. F. Austin to S. M. Williams, June 20, 1832, Samuel May Williams Papers, Rosenberg Library, Galveston; John Austin to José Antonio Mexía, July 18, 1832, in Eugene C. Barker, ed., *The Austin Papers*, 2:818–20, hereafter cited as *Austin Papers*.

persecute the settlers, according to Foote, and the "unprincipled *renegade*" arrested civilians without cause and then treated the prisoners with "extraordinary cruelty." The "faithless miscreant [Bradburn] . . . opened a treacherous fire" on the residents of Anahuac, who had negotiated an armistice, and "this odious breach of faith" caused the Texans to attack the fort.[2]

Subsequent nineteenth-century writers used less flamboyant language but perpetuated the view that Bradburn was unreasonable and capricious in his treatment of the settlers. Even after participants in the glorious deeds of the 1830s passed from the scene, their views tended to dominate scholarly writing in the early twentieth century.[3]

Edna Rowe, a graduate student in the University of Texas in 1900, wrote her master's thesis about the events at Anahuac. Three years later her seminal study appeared in the *Quarterly of the Texas State Historical Association* as "The Disturbances at Anahuac in 1832." The only primary sources available at the time were the Béxar Archives, the Nacogdoches Archives, and the papers of Stephen F. Austin, all unpublished,

[2] Henry Stuart Foote, *Texas and the Texans; or, Advance of the Anglo-Americans to the South-west*, 2:14–18.

[3] Henderson Yoakum, *History of Texas from Its First Settlement in 1685 to Its Annexation to the United States in 1846*, 2:290–91; Willard Richardson, "History of Galveston," and Frank W. Johnson, "Further Account by Col. F. W. Johnson of the First Breaking Out of Hostilities," both in *The Texas Almanac for 1859*, in James Day, comp., *The Texas Almanac, 1857–1873: A Compendium of Texas History*, pp. 137, 181–83; J. M. Morphis, *History of Texas*, pp. 20–21; John J. Linn, *Reminiscences of Fifty Years in Texas*, pp. 16–17; Homer S. Thrall, *A Pictorial History of Texas from the Earliest Visits of European Adventurers to A.D. 1879*, p. 179; Hubert Howe Bancroft, *History of the North Mexican States and Texas*, 2:118–19; John Henry Brown, *History of Texas from 1685 to 1892* . . . , pp. 167–69.

poorly arranged, and lacking indexes. Rowe therefore borrowed heavily from published accounts from the nineteenth century and, influenced by the strong rhetoric in those books, blamed Bradburn for all of the trouble. He was "naturally . . . overbearing," and his administration at Anahuac was "unwise" and "absolute tyranny" when he "arbitrarily" arrested colonists. Rowe also used Vicente Filisola's *Memorias para la historia de la guerra de Tejas*, a two-volume work published in 1848 and 1849, which supplied many details about the Mexican political scene and Bradburn's activities. Filisola wrote his account in the late 1830s, using files available to him as commandant general of the Eastern Interior States, including letters and a report from Bradburn to his military superior in 1832.[4]

Twenty years later Eugene Campbell Barker, teacher and editor of the *Quarterly*, published his biography of Stephen F. Austin. By that time more source material was available for scholarly research, such as transcripts from various Mexican archives and the collections of papers belonging to Mirabeau Buonaparte Lamar and Samuel May Williams. Although Barker cited a letter from Austin to Manuel de Mier y Terán from the Wagner Western America Collection, at Yale University, he overlooked a very

[4]Edna Rowe, "The Disturbances at Anahuac in 1832," *Quarterly of the Texas State Historical Association* 6 (April, 1903):265–99. Vicente Filisola, *Memorias para la historia de la guerra de Tejas* . . . . A draft of Bradburn's report, "Memoria del Coronel Juan Davis Bradburn sobre los acontecimientos de Anáhuac, 1831–1832," is in the Henry R. Wagner Texas and Middle West Collection of the Beinecke Rare Book and Manuscript Library, Yale University; translated typescript copies are in the Sam Houston Regional Library and Research Center, Liberty, Texas, and a composite translation is given in Appendix 1, below; the report is cited hereafter as "Bradburn Memorial."

important document in that archive, Bradburn's draft of his "Memoria," which gives his version of the events at Anahuac (see Appendix 1). Admittedly a self-serving defense of his conduct as commander of the Texas garrison, it nevertheless challenges the traditional accounts. If Barker had read it, he might have modified his statements about Bradburn in chapter 12 of his biography of Austin.[5]

"Unfortunately," he begins there, "an American, Colonel John Davis Bradburn, was stationed at the head of Galveston Bay." Bradburn was "irascible, arbitrary, and injudicious. His pretentiousness made him the butt of practical jokes and ridicule, which, lacking the good sense to ignore, he sought to punish with undue severity and very questionable authority." To illustrate this contention, Barker quoted from Austin's letter to Williams saying that Bradburn was "half crazy part of his time." That single citation fails to document adequately Barker's description of Bradburn, but his evaluation of the colonel became the accepted source for subsequent monographs and textbooks.[6]

One modern college text calls Bradburn a "stubborn, tactless Kentuckian" whose "first serious offense" against the Texans was his arrest of a state land commissioner. Another volume labels the colonel "an adventurer from Kentucky" who antagonized the settlers by his "haughty attitude and high-handed tactics." A popular junior-high-school textbook pub-

[5] Eugene C. Barker, *The Life of Stephen F. Austin: Founder of Texas, 1793–1836*, p. 329.
[6] Ibid., p. 322.

[17]

lished in 1978 claims that Bradburn was stubborn and filled with pride and that his actions were very foolish; moreover, the textbook claims, he "broke every rule that a good military leader should follow." A popular history published in 1969 describes the colonel as "a peculiarly arrogant officer" who ignored all civil authority and treated all civilians with contempt.[7]

Who, then, was this incompetent, half-crazy, despotic, arbitrary man who arrested innocent civilians and trampled on their rights? How could such a wretched, unprincipled renegade become the commander of the garrison at Anahuac? Why did he persecute the Texans? Was he really pretentious and irascible, haughty and high-handed?

In the following pages I reappraise the sources and, with additional research, revise the dark legend that has enveloped Bradburn. Instead of a capricious villain, the colonel emerges, not totally without blemish, as a career officer in the Mexican army who was following orders to enforce national laws that were unpopular among states'-rights-minded Anglo-Texans. Bradburn was not democratic, because for more than twenty years he had been giving and receiving orders in the military, but he was not a despot.

[7] Rupert N. Richardson et al., *Texas: The Lone Star State*, pp. 72–73; Seymour V. Conner, *Texas: A History*, p. 93; Jim B. Pearson, Ben Procter, et al., *Texas: The Land and the People*, pp. 263–64; T. R. Fehrenbach, *Lone Star: A History of Texas and Texans*, p. 170.

The Man

RECONSTRUCTING the life of Juan Davis Bradburn, the name that he used for the last twenty-five years of his life, presents a challenge to the researcher. His family was not prominent enough to appear in county histories of the various places they lived, nor are deed records, marriage records, or court minutes of help because the names of his ancestors remain unknown. His only child, a son, became a priest in Mexico, and if any family documents exist, they have yet to be discovered. A nephew, William P. Bradburn, lived in LaGrange, Texas, for two years after an unsuccessful effort in 1842 to claim a portion of Bradburn's estate along the Rio Grande in the state of Tamaulipas. The nephew left for Louisiana, where he lived from 1845 to 1864, but if he revealed any details about his uncle, they are not recorded.[1] Thus Bradburn's story rests

---

[1] William P. Bradburn, nephew of the colonel, lived in Texas from 1843 to 1845 and published a newspaper in LaGrange. The census records show that in 1850, when he was thirty-six, he lived in Iberville Parish, Louisiana, with his wife, age seventeen, had no children, was a native of Tennessee, and was an editor. He edited and published the *Southern Sentinel* in Plaquemine from 1848 to 1858, when it merged with the *Iberville Gazette*, and he remained in charge of the *Gazette and Sentinel* through at least 1861. See Walter Prescott Webb et al., eds., *The Handbook of Texas,*

on the few letters, diaries, and memoirs that mention him and on the occasional documents discovered in the United States and Mexico that record his activities.

According to Mexican military records, Bradburn was born in 1787 in Richmond, Virginia; however, research in Henrico County and nearby counties failed to reveal the presence of any Bradburns. Most likely the Bradburns lived in one of the frontier counties along the Blue Ridge or southwest of the James River, areas that attracted many Scotch-Irish families. Perhaps Bradburn, when enrolling in the Mexican army, answered with the name of the state capital instead of the county seat when asked what town had jurisdiction over his birthplace.[2] In any event, the Virginia Bradburns traveled through the Cumberland Gap into Kentucky, as did large numbers of other Virginia residents in the 1790s.

A contemporary of Bradburn in Anahuac, William B. Scates, placed the Bradburn family in Christian County, Kentucky, after 1800, and the United States census of 1810 confirms the statement. A William C. Bradburn, recorded as over forty-five years of age, and John, single, between sixteen and twenty-six, appear in the census rolls—seemingly the future colonel (who would have been twenty-three) and his father. Scates, writing in 1871, when he was seventy

---

1:203–204; United States Census, 1850, Iberville Parish, no. 95, p. 313; *Louisiana Newspapers, 1794–1940*, pp. 681, 694. Julia Sinks, in "Editors and Newspapers of Fayette County," *Quarterly of the Texas State Historical Association* 1 (July, 1897):34, says that William P. was to inherit his uncle's estate but that the colonel's death in 1842 interrupted the paper work.

[2] Manuel Mestre Ghigliazza, comp., *Efemérides biográficas*, p. 33.

years old, said that he had lived near the Bradburns and that the two sons of the family, John and William, became merchants in Springfield, Tennessee, "just across" the Kentucky border on the road to Nashville. These facts plus an 1814 county tax roll listing the father's 111 acres on the Little River, are the only records available, because the Christian County Court House burned in the 1860s.[3]

Scates, seeking to disparage Bradburn in his memoir of 1871, said that the brothers once stole some slaves, for which crime they were jailed in Maury County, Tennessee. As he recalled, the brothers escaped, and one drowned in the nearby Duck River, while the other went to Mexico. Scates was only partly right. A William Bradburn drowned in the Duck about June 11, 1816, and the county court provided a pauper's coffin for him. The two men who escaped from the jail on the night of June 10 were not the Bradburns, however; one was accused of murder and the other of horse theft. An account of the incident appeared in the August 1, 1816, *Columbia Chronicle*—the only issue of 1816 that still exists—but there is no mention of the Bradburns or of an unnamed accomplice. While it appears that Bradburn's brother may have died under peculiar circumstances, the records fail to implicate the colonel in any way or to support Scates's selective account a half century later.[4]

[3]United States Census, 1810, Christian County, Kentucky; William B. Scates, "Early History of Anahuac," in *The Texas Almanac for 1873,* in Day, comp., *The Texas Almanac, 1857–1873,* pp. 681–82; Christian County, Kentucky, Tax Roll, 1814.

[4]Scates, "Early History of Anahuac," pp. 681–82; Jill Knight Garrett, *Maury County Cousins,* 2:274; Jill Knight Garrett, *Maury County,*

While there is no documentation of Bradburn's trading activities, one can assume that he traveled the Natchez Trace southwest from Nashville to the Mississippi River and perhaps beyond, into Louisiana. Other adventuresome young men were engaged in such enterprises, and Bradburn's election as an officer in the Louisiana militia at Natchitoches in 1814 suggests that he was well known to residents of the neighborhood. By 1812 such trading trips would have exposed him to the activities of refugee Mexican patriots and their American supporters who were actively seeking aid in the Mississippi Valley to further the cause of Mexican independence from Spain. Guerrilla activities after 1810 kept Mexico in turmoil for a decade, and from time to time refugees and agents crowded cities in Louisiana. New Orleans merchants in particular offered support for the rebels in the hope that an independent Mexico would open trade with the United States. Mexico was a potentially rich market traditionally forbidden to foreigners by Spain.

The first major filibustering expedition organized in Louisiana was that of José Bernardo Gutiérrez de Lara, a refugee from the Rio Grande, and Augustus W. Magee, a former officer in the United States Army. Bradburn had ample opportunity to join the undertaking, though his name does not appear in any of the accounts. The force numbered somewhere

Tennessee, Newspaper Abstracts, 1810–1844, p. 274. It is possible that Scates confused the Bradburns with William and Frank Hardin, who fled Maury County in 1825 to avoid an indictment for murder and settled in the Atascosita community. See Webb et al., eds., *Handbook of Texas*, 1:768–69.

between 500 and 2,000 volunteers, but efforts to list participants have resulted in perhaps 125 positive identifications.[5] All who joined the expedition expected financial reward and, if not beauty and booty, at least a substantial tract of land in Texas. Only circumstantial evidence suggests that Bradburn took part in the undertaking. Many of those who elected him third lieutenant in Natchitoches in 1814 were members of the 1812 expedition that captured Nacogdoches and La Bahía. It seems logical that these adventurers would elect the Kentuckian only if he had won their respect during previous military engagements. Moreover, after the close of the War of 1812, Bradburn aligned himself with Henry Perry and other participants of the Gutiérrez-Magee expedition in a new filibustering attack on Texas and was given a command. Thus it seems obvious that he had won a military reputation among his fellows.

While Gutiérrez was the titular head of the invasion of Nacogdoches in August, 1812, Magee was the commander of the American volunteers. Leaving Natchitoches in small "hunting" parties, the filibusters captured Nacogdoches in August, La Bahía in November, and Béxar in March, 1813. Magee died, some of the Mexican patriots committed atrocities in the name of revenge, and many of the Americans became disgusted and returned home. The royalist

[5] Harris Gaylord Warren, *The Sword Was Their Passport: A History of American Filibustering in the Mexican Revolution*, pp. 30, 35–36; Linda Ericson Devereaux, "The Gutierrez-Magee Expedition," *Texana* 11 (1973): 52–73; William McLane, "William McLane's Narrative of the Magee-Gutierrez Expedition, 1812–1813," ed. William P. Walker, *Southwestern Historical Quarterly* 66 (April, 1963):580–88.

army delivered a stunning blow to the remaining republican force at the Medina River west of Béxar in August, 1813, forcing the survivors to flee to Louisiana.

Smarting at their defeat on the Medina, about 400 refugees gathered in Natchitoches in September, 1813, and made plans to organize another expedition that would honor previous contracts and obligations. Rival groups vied for financing, and six months elapsed before parties started toward Nacogdoches. Continued bickering among the leaders soon caused the merchants to withdraw financial support, and at the end of the summer, one year after the defeat on the Medina, most of the adventurers returned to Natchitoches to await further developments. These men, including Bradburn, were available for the militia call in December, 1814, when the British threatened to invade New Orleans.[6]

Bradburn and a younger brother (or perhaps a nephew or cousin), Richard D. Bradburn, enrolled in Captain Jean Louis Buard's company, the only company of the Eighteenth Louisiana Regiment to have a full complement of men. By the order of Governor William C. C. Claiborne issued on August 6, 1814, each company in the Louisiana militia was to have a captain, a first lieutenant, 2 second lieutenants, 4 sergeants, 4 corporals, a drummer and fifer, and 90 privates—a total of 104 men. While Richard enrolled as

---

[6]"Information from Capt. Gaines, 1835," in Charles Adams Gulick, Jr., et al., eds., *The Papers of Mirabeau Buonaparte Lamar* 1:284; hereafter cited as *Lamar Papers*; Warren, *The Sword Was Their Passport*, pp. 65, 81, 89–95, 115–16.

a private, Juan Davis Bradburn was elected third lieutenant, the rank probably indicating that he was the second of the two second lieutenants. The remaining companies from Natchitoches Parish were undermanned, and the one commanded by Francisco Alvarado was composed of native Mexicans, all refugees from Texas. The Eighteenth Regiment joined the Seventeenth, from Rapides Parish, and the Nineteenth, from Ouachita. The combined roster included several men later associated with Texas: James and Reason Bowie, Joshua Childs, John Durst, Warren D. C. Hall, his brother John W. Hall, John Latham, and William Little. All were privates except Warren Hall, who was made a corporal. Bradburn outranked them all.[7]

The combined units left for New Orleans on January 8, 1815—the same day that Andrew Jackson defeated the British—and arrived in the Crescent City on January 24, sixteen days later. The Eighteenth Regiment remained in the city until March 11, when most of the militia units returned home. For his two months and twenty-four days of service 3d Lt. Bradburn collected $63.80 plus a rations allowance of $32.70, a total of $96.50, while Richard received $22.19.[8]

New Orleans remained full of former filibuster-

[7] Powell A. Casey, *Louisiana in the War of 1812*, pp. 15, 39; see also Marion John Bennett Pierson, comp., *Louisiana Soldiers in the War of 1812*, p. 16.

[8] Pierson, comp., *Louisiana Soldiers in the War of 1812*, p. 16; United States Compiled Military Service Records, Records of the Adjutant General's Office, 1780–1917, Record Group 94, Volunteer Organizations [War of 1812], 17th, 18th, and 19th Consolidated Regiment, Louisiana Militia, Caption Cards.

ers, including Gutiérrez de Lara, José Alvarez de Toledo, and Henry Perry, who joined with Juan Pablo Anaya, a representative of one faction of the insurgent cause, to make new plans for invading Mexican territory. All had served with Jackson during the recent British invasion and were ready for further adventures.[9] Rumors and counterrumors kept alive the filibusterers' hopes as plans were made and then discarded.

After his discharge Bradburn became associated with Anaya and Perry in a plan to capture La Bahía while Gutiérrez raised a force that would follow the same route as that of 1812. The two groups would join forces at La Bahía to attack San Antonio. After thus securing the northern frontier, the republicans would move south to join creole insurgents. Perry had won fame in June, 1813, when he took command of the American wing of the Gutiérrez expedition in Béxar and defeated a royalist force. Anaya commissioned him a colonel in the Republican Army of Mexico, and in July, 1815, inflammatory notices appeared over his signature in New Orleans newspapers urging those who wanted "distinction" and "glorious rewards" to rendezvous at Belle Isle, near the mouth of the Atchafalaya River, for "the favorable moment" had arrived for attacking La Bahía, which, the notices predicted, would fall easily. This open violation of the Neutrality Act of 1794 stimulated the Spanish minister in Washington, D.C., to demand action. President James Madison issued an executive order for an im-

[9] Warren, *The Sword Was Their Passport*, pp. 112–14; Mirabeau B. Lamar, "Early Settlement of Texas," in *Lamar Papers*, 6:443.

mediate cessation of unfriendly activity against Spanish dominions. The order was noticed but not enforced in the Crescent City, where there was much sympathy for the cause.[10] Perry assembled about 300 volunteers, including Warren D. C. Hall, at the staging area, but was unable to secure sufficient funds to transport the men to Copano Bay. As an alternative in November he chartered a small vessel to take the men to Galveston Bay. The first contingent landed on the narrow peninsula northeast of Galveston Island. The strategic point offered certain advantages that the island did not: wood and fresh water were readily available, and Indian trails connected with both the Sabine River and the Atascosito Road, an old Indian trail used by smugglers, which stretched from Opelousas, Louisiana, to La Bahía. As yet unnamed, the point would become Bolivar in 1816, when one of the South American liberator's lieutenants, Luís de Aury, arrived.

A second voyage from Belle Isle ended in a disaster when the schooner foundered at the entrance to Galveston Bay and 60 men were drowned and supplies lost.[11] Undaunted, Perry postponed his invasion plans and ordered the force inland to seek a better site for a permanent camp while he secured rein-

[10] Warren, *The Sword Was Their Passport*, pp. 21, 62–64, 122–24, 126; *Niles' Weekly Register* 9 (September 16, 1815): 33; unsigned letter to Vicente Guerrero, April 27, 1821, Juan E. Hernández y Dávalos Manuscript Collection, Benson Latin American Collection, University of Texas at Austin. Warren D. C. Hall says that Perry rendezvoused on a timbered island on the west side of Vermilion Bay called Chat-au-Tigre. From there Perry moved his force to Bolívar in September, 1815. See Charles W. Hayes, *Galveston: History of the Island and the City*, 1:17–18.

[11] Warren, *The Sword Was Their Passport*, pp. 130–31; Hayes, *Galveston*, 1:19; *Lamar Papers*, 6:433.

forcements from Louisiana. He settled on a high bluff overlooking the mouth of the Trinity River in the northeastern portion of upper Galveston Bay, where there was ample wood and water. The site was known as Perry's Point from 1815 to 1831, when Bradburn, acting on superior orders, named it Anahuac in honor of the ancient center of the Aztecs.

Perry ordered Bradburn, now ranked sergeant major, and ten or twelve volunteers to Nacogdoches to receive recruits and supplies coming over the road from Natchitoches. One of Bradburn's assignments was to raise the six cannons abandoned in the Sabine River in 1814 by John Smith T, one of the rival leaders of the aborted plan to reinvade Texas. A trader reported that he saw Bradburn in Nacogdoches in December, 1815, and that he had already recovered one four-pounder from the river. Whether he salvaged the remaining cannons is unknown, but he remained in the vicinity until March, 1816, when a Spanish patrol learned that there were "400 vagabonds" in Nacogdoches, doubtless an exaggeration. All were gone by June, reportedly to Galveston Island, where a large force was assembling, according to Spanish informants.[12]

About March, 1816, Perry joined forces with Luís de Aury, who had occupied Galveston Island. Named commodore of the invasion fleet and also governor of the province of Texas by the revolutionary

[12] Deposition of Edmund Quirk, February 12, 1816; Governor of Texas to Commandant Genéral, March 26, 1816; Juan de Casteñeda to Governor Mariano Varela, June 30, 1816, Robert Bruce Blake Research Collection, Texas History Center, Houston Public Library, Houston, Supplement 8, pp. 216–21, 123, 124; hereafter cited as Blake Collection.

Mexican government in exile in New Orleans, Aury began preparing for the intended assault on La Bahía. Perry agreed to commit his men with the understanding that he would be in charge of the land force. As usual, unexpected delays in securing funds postponed the attack, and Aury's men, including 200 blacks from Haiti, spent their time salvaging wrecks and constructing a fort, tasks not entirely to their liking. Mutiny and desertions reduced the army to about 200 men in September.[13]

At this juncture Francisco Xavier Mina arrived at Galveston on November 22, 1816, with men, supplies, and a plan to invade Mexico near Tampico and join insurgent leaders in the interior in an effort to end the seven-year struggle against Spain. A native of Navarre, in the Spanish Pyrenees, Mina had become a brilliant guerrilla leader fighting the French occupation of his homeland in 1808. When the exiled King Ferdinand VII resumed the Spanish throne in 1814, however, he refused to honor reforms adopted by the Spanish cortes (parliament) during his absence, and Mina, along with other liberal republicans, fled the country and plotted to overthrow the Spanish Empire. He arrived in the United States in 1816 and actively recruited support in the major eastern cities in spite of protests from the Spanish minister. A charismatic leader, Mina attracted many American adventurers, including Col. Guilford Dudley Young, a veteran of the War of 1812, who was to recruit and command Americans. Despite protests Mina's flotilla

[13] Warren, *The Sword Was Their Passport*, pp. 139–45; *Lamar Papers*, 6:444.

slipped out of the Atlantic ports and reached Galveston with about 140 officers and men.[14]

Aury reluctantly welcomed the rival commander, but their different goals (attacking Texas posts or Tampico) and intrigue among lesser officers caused discord. Aury proposed to move his camp to Matagorda Bay, but Henry Perry objected, and the two reached a compromise: all volunteers would be released from previous commitments and could choose between the Aury and the Mina expeditions. Already attracted to Mina, Perry, Bradburn, Young, and most of the Anglo-American filibusterers sided with Mina, and they began preparing for the assault on the Tamaulipas coast in March, 1817.[15]

The expedition left Galveston on April 7 with at least eight vessels and about 350 men and about two weeks later arrived at the mouth of the Santander River, midway between the Rio Grande and Tampico. The force easily captured Soto la Marina, about thirty miles inland, and the royalist force withdrew from the vicinity. The brilliant but temperamental Perry became disenchanted with Mina, and he and about 50 supporters started overland for Texas, where they met their deaths at La Bahía in a quixotic and unnecessary attack.[16]

Bradburn, however, chose to stay with Mina and rose to second-in-command of the American wing, under Col. Young. Mina, skilled in guerrilla tactics, had difficulty directing a long campaign and stockpil-

[14] Warren, *The Sword Was Their Passport*, pp. 146–54, 158–60.
[15] Ibid., pp. 160–61.
[16] Ibid., pp. 166–71; *Lamar Papers*, 6:445–47.

ing supplies, and gradually many of his troops drifted away. He ordered the remaining army into the interior and abandoned Soto la Marina to the royalists. Mina and his followers finally reached Fort Sombrero, an insurgent stronghold in Guanajuato, where they joined Pedro Moreno. The combined force included about 650 fighting men and 250 peasants, including women and children, within the compound. On July 30 a royalist force of 3,500 men and ten pieces of artillery appeared outside the fort and commenced a siege that lasted almost three weeks. Defiant at first, Mina raised the red flag that signaled "No quarter," but soon the insurgents were suffering from lack of water and supplies, and it appeared that nearby patriots would not relieve the fort. Local *caudillos* resented Mina because he was a *gachupín*, a native-born Spaniard, and therefore suspect.[17]

While Mina was unsuccessfully seeking aid, those inside the fort were reduced to eating horses, dogs, and weeds, and they finally sent out a white flag to inquire what terms the enemy would offer. Since 1816 generous royal pardons had been given to insurgent leaders in an effort to end the civil war and reduce carnage on both sides, and many had taken advantage of the chance to cease fighting. This policy had been one of the factors that prevented Mina from recruiting aid for the cause of independence. Col. Young, Bradburn, and the other Americans were dismayed when the messenger returned: native Mex-

[17] Warren, *The Sword Was Their Passport*, pp. 169–71; John Anthony Caruso, *The Liberators of Mexico*, p. 155; William Davis Robinson, *Memoirs of the Mexican Revolution*, 193–200.

icans would receive amnesty, but all foreigners would surrender at discretion, which meant that, if he chose, the royalist commander could shoot them as filibusterers. That night a royalist attack was barely repulsed, and when Young mounted the wall to observe the Spanish retreat, a cannonball struck him, killing him instantly.[18]

Bradburn, as lieutenant colonel, succeeded Young in command of the American contingent. His only option was to evacuate as soon as possible, and all day on August 19 the men buried or destroyed supplies that might be of use to the enemy. Most difficult of all was saying good-bye to comrades too feeble to descend the rocky ravine on their own. For some reason the Mexican commander allowed the women and children to depart first that night. Soon children became separated from their mothers, and the cries of both alerted the enemy pickets. Within minutes the entire area was a mass of confusion, and the desperate rebels struck out singly or in small groups. Those unfamiliar with the terrain were doomed when daylight came. The Spanish cavalrymen rode them down, cutting them to pieces with their sabers. Of the 200 defenders remaining in the fort on August 19, possibly one-fourth escaped by luck or the aid of a local guide. Among the escapees was Bradburn, but we have no details explaining his good fortune.[19]

Bradburn made his way south to the valleys along the border of Guanajuato and San Luis Potosí, where he

[18] Robinson, *Memoirs*, pp. 200–204.
[19] Ibid., pp. 204–207.

found sympathizers to the cause. There he also learned of Mina's death on November 11, 1817; Mina had been captured while planning an attack on the town of Guanajuato and sentenced to die before a firing squad. Bradburn became a leader in organizing local patriot forces and helped establish an armory and a powder factory. Spanish offers of royal pardons continued to weaken the insurgent armies, and many rebel chieftains deserted and accepted commands in the royal army, the reward promised for defecting. Bradburn, however, held fast even when the Spaniards destroyed his powder mill near Chucándiro early in 1818. He then retreated south toward Acapulco, where rebel leaders Vicente Guerrero and Pedro Ascensio were carrying on the struggle for independence.[20]

Guerrero, a mestizo peasant who lacked the polish that had attracted many American recruits to Mina, offended a number of the volunteers with his cruelty. Charges of corruption also antagonized the idealistic young Americans, but Bradburn remained loyal to the cause and to Guerrero during 1819. Some of his American colleagues accepted royal pardons, and at the instigation of the Spanish viceroy one of them wrote Bradburn begging him to abandon the "vile" insurgents who were "without honor, talent or even common politeness" and surrender himself to the "legitimate" government. Referring to Guerrero's forces as a "gang of thieves," Bradburn's former colleague warned that he and "his party" were hated by

[20] José María Miquel i Vergés, *Diccionario de insurgentes*, p. 85; Hubert Howe Bancroft, *The History of Mexico, 1804–1824*, 4:694.

all and did not command the respect Mina had won. The colonel expressed astonishment that his friend believed Spanish propaganda and wrote that he himself refused to listen to such "improper observations."[21]

Bradburn's activities with Guerrero are undocumented, but evidently the mestizo leader trusted him. At one point, however, Bradburn intervened with Guerrero's order to shoot some royalist officers taken prisoner, but whether that caused a breach is unknown. His intervention to save the lives of the officers earned Bradburn the respect of Agustín Iturbide, commander of the royalist forces fighting Guerrero, and launched the colonel on his career as a Mexican officer. Bradburn's ultimate defection from the insurgent army in December, 1820, is explained by Mexican historians as weariness with the conflict, but one Mexican source says that he changed sides with Guerrero's consent, going as a spy into the royalist camp.[22]

One month after accepting a Spanish pardon from Iturbide, Bradburn was serving as an intermediary between his new leader and Guerrero, a seemingly delicate task unless Guerrero had approved his leaving the rebel cause. With his unique connections with each side Bradburn could transmit

[21] J. M. Hebb to J. D. Bradburn April 14, 1819; J. D. Bradburn to J. M. Hebb, March 20, 1819, Papeles de Estado, Mexico, Legajo 14, no. 21, Archivo General de las Indias, Sevilla, William E. Dunn transcripts, Barker History Center, University of Texas at Austin. "Hebb" is identified as Isaac W. Webb in Harris Gaylord Warren, "The Origin of General Mina's Invasion of Mexico," *Southwestern Historical Quarterly* 42 (July, 1938):4, n. 9.

[22] *Diccionario Porrúa*, 4th ed., p. 625; Leopoldo Zamora Plowes, *Quince Unas y Casanova aventureros*, p. 465.

both verbal and written communications from Iturbide to the rebels, urging them to end the war by forming an alliance of all native Mexicans to expel the Spanish army and organize a new government.[23]

Iturbide had joined the army as a cadet in 1797 at the age of fifteen, and after the outbreak of the revolution in 1810 he pursued rebel leaders efficiently and cruelly. Rewarded for his diligence, he nevertheless believed that his fortune and career were advancing too slowly and blamed it on the fact that he was a creole (a Spaniard born in Mexico). His frustration increased in 1816, when he had to retire because of public complaints about his overzealous prosecution of his duties. In November, 1820, still seething with resentment against peninsular Spaniards, Iturbide accepted a return to active duty. His assignment was to persuade or force the last two rebel *jefes*, Guerrero and Ascencio, to accept pardons and end the bloodshed.

Inspired by Napoleon and Simón Bolívar, Iturbide secretly dreamed about becoming the liberator of Mexico, and during his forced retirement he had considered ways that might be accomplished. He accepted the November commission with the intent of betraying the Spanish authorities by appealing to all native Mexicans to unite against the *peninsulares*. His ideas, promulgated as the Plan de Iguala in February, 1821, included a statement declaring Mexico separated from Spain, but also declaring that, instead of a republic, the country would be a constitutional mon-

---

[23] Zamaro Plowes, *Quince Unas*, p. 465. See also Lucas Alamán, *Historia de Méjico desde . . . el año de 1808 hasta la época presente*, 5:87–92.

archy ruled either by Bourbon prince or by a native Mexican surrogate. The Roman Catholic church would remain the established religion, and full citizenship would be extended to all natives, as well as to any foreigners and Spaniards who cared to declare their loyalty. While appealing to every faction, the scheme pleased none totally. Bradburn, now a colonel in the royalist army, opened negotiations with Guerrero in January, and on March 14, the insurgents endorsed the plan.[24]

Iturbide quickly subverted the army by offering defecting officers equal or higher rank in the Army of the Three Guarantees, as the combined force of royalist deserters and former patriots was called. In August, 1821, the viceroy signed the treaty recognizing the separation of Mexico and Spain, and most royalist military commanders immediately surrendered except the commander in the capital, who held out until September. Bradburn participated in the bloody fighting in Mexico City that preceded the capitulation and doubtless took part in the grand victory parade through *la ciudad*.[25]

For the next eight months elected deputies, most of whom were unfamiliar with either republican principles or democratic processes, struggled to create a government that would satisfy conservative monarchists on the one side and liberal reformers on the other. Iturbide ended the confusion in April, 1822, by accepting a call to become Emperor Agustín I, but

[24] William Spence Robertson, *Iturbide of Mexico*, pp. 8, 32–37, 48, 50–65.
[25] Ibid., pp. 204, 214, 221.

his extravagant reign lasted only one year, after which one of his associates, Antonio López de Santa Anna, led his own revolt, calling for a republic. Guerrero and other former insurgents who had been left out of Iturbide's empire joined Santa Anna and forced the "liberator" to sail for Europe and exile. While Iturbide remained in power, however, Bradburn prospered. In 1822 the emperor sent him to Washington, D.C., as a courier, and he returned on the schooner *Iguala*, the first warship in the Mexican navy, just purchased in the United States. Bradburn brought the good news that the United States planned to recognize the independence of all the Latin-American republics, a step confirmed for Mexico by Congress in December, 1822. As Iturbide's aide Bradburn moved in Mexico City society, and Augustín I arranged a suitable marriage for him to a "girl of good family."[26] At the age of thirty-four Bradburn was ready to settle down, and since he had fought so long for Mexican independence, a Mexican wife with property seemed natural and sensible.

María Josefa Hurtado de Mendoza y Caballero de los Olivos was the fifth Marquise de Ciría and the fifteenth Marshal of Castilla, titles granted to worthy Spaniards by the king. Her brother Agustín Hurtado was the ninth Count of the Valley of Orizaba, a uniquely Mexican title. In 1821 he had married the sister of Mariano Paredes y Arrillaga, who was destined to be briefly president of the Republic of Mexico in 1846. The Hurtado family owned a large tract

[26] Miquel i Vergés, *Diccionario de insurgentes*, p. 85; Alamán, *Historia*, 5:541.

near the Zócalo and the cathedral, and their residence was known as the Casa de Azulejos (House of Tiles), which in the twentieth century became Sanborn's Restaurant. Other Hurtado property included the Church Foundation of the Monastery and Church of San Diego, in Colón Street, on a tract that ultimately descended to Bradburn's only son.[27]

One can imagine the dismay that Bradburn and his wife felt when the empire collapsed. Having been granted Mexican citizenship along with his commission, Bradburn somehow managed to survive the political changes for the next decade. The Army of the Three Guarantees remained large, primarily because it represented the only means of rewarding the supporters of independence; more than one half of the men in the army were officers. While most of the generals were native Mexicans, many of the other officers were of foreign birth, among them Bradburn and his colleague from the Mina expedition Adrian Woll, a native of Belgium. Once the Federalists (those favoring a weak central government and strong state governments) won ascendancy over the conservative Centralists in 1824, the army was somewhat reduced, but Bradburn kept his rank by carefully cultivating those men who would see that he retained his sinecure. Hence Bradburn associated himself with Nicolás Bravo, Manuel de Mier y Terán, and Anastasio

[27]Julio de Atienza, *Títulos nobiliarios hispano americanos*, p. 134; Guillermo S. Fernández de Recas, *Mayorazgos de la Nueva España*, p. 168; Manuel Rivera Cambas, *México pintoresco, artístico & monumental*, 1:230–32, photocopy pages trans. John V. Clay and Alan Probert, Wallisville Heritage Park Archives, Wallisville, Texas.

Bustamante, all of whom became conservative Centralists after 1824. While Bravo and Mier y Terán had supported the independence movement in its early stages, they had accepted royal amnesty by 1817, and they maintained a low profile until 1822, when they emerged as conservatives. Bustamante, on the other hand, remained a Spanish officer until 1821, when he joined Iturbide, understanding that a monarchy was the goal. The collapse of the empire failed to convert Bustamante to the ideal of a republic, and he remained a firm Centralist the rest of his life.[28]

Citizens of the United States with business in Mexico in 1822 sought Bradburn's influence even before Iturbide became emperor. Andrew Erwin and Robert Leftwich, investors in the Texas Association of Nashville, asked him to endorse the petition that they intended to place before Congress requesting a colonization contract to settle families in Texas. Bradburn probably knew Leftwich, who had lived in Logan County, Kentucky, in 1808, and perhaps Erwin, a well-known trader in central Tennessee. Bradburn said in his endorsement that he knew many of the seventy investors who had signed the petition and also the governor of Tennessee, William Carroll, who had signed the memorial.[29]

[28] T. R. Fehrenbach, *Fire and Blood: A History of Mexico*, pp. 365–66, 368, 390.
[29] J. D. Bradburn to Juan Pablo Anaya, May 8, 1822, Everett B. Graff Collection, Newberry Library, Chicago. The translated letter also appears in Malcom D. McLean, comp. and ed., *Papers Concerning Robertson's Colony in Texas*, 1:377–378; for a full account of the Texas Association and its participants see 1:xli–lxix, 364–96, 422–45.

Many of these men belonged to the Masonic fraternity, and Bradburn was a member of the Royal Arch chapter in Mexico City. In his endorsement of the project, addressed to Juan Pablo Anaya, his former associate in New Orleans, now a cabinet minister, Bradburn said that he was "particularly" well acquainted with the governor, a word that was often used between members of the Masonic movement to introduce brothers. Masonry became a political and diplomatic issue in Mexico when United States Chargé d'Affaires Joel R. Poinsett secured York Rite charters from the United States for his friends in the Federalist party. Politics divided Mexican Masons into two camps. The Centralists—primarily generals, church officials, and large landowners—affiliated with the Scottish Rite branch and received their charters through the British minister. The Federalists— state-oriented republicans and liberal reformers— joined the York Rite lodges. Some of the refugees in New Orleans in 1816 secured support from local lodges, and the Grand Lodge of Louisiana chartered Los Amigos Reunidos in Vera Cruz the same year. It is possible that Bradburn and Anaya were members of a New Orleans lodge, but the records of the Grand Lodge of Louisiana were destroyed by fire, and the matter is mere conjecture.[30]

Bradburn's endorsement of the Tennessean's petition failed to be of immediate use because of the coronation of Iturbide in June, 1822, and the subse-

[30] James David Carter, *Masonry in Texas: Background, History, and Influence to 1846*, pp. 221, 243, 191.

quent political turmoil that destroyed the Mexican Congress prevented action. After Iturbide was exiled and Congress was reinstalled, the legislators decided that granting colonization contracts was a matter for each state to decide. The Tennessee associates had to wait for the organization of the state of Coahuila-Texas. Congress united the dissimilar pair in 1824, locating the capital in Saltillo until such time as Texas had the requisite population for statehood. The petitioners finally received their empresario contract in 1825 without any help from Bradburn.

Even after Iturbide's departure Bradburn appeared to have influence with the authorities. In August, 1824, he certified that Col. Benjamin Rush Milam had come to Texas with insurgent leader José Félix Trespalacios; the pair arrived in the capital in November, 1821, and in July, 1822, Milam was arrested by Iturbide and banished without receiving compensation for his service during the past three years. In 1824, Milam wanted Congress to reward him with an empresario grant in extreme northeastern Texas, but he too had to resubmit his petition to the legislature of Coahuila-Texas. It was granted in 1826 in conjunction with another petition.[31] Only Stephen F. Austin received a colonizaton contract from the imperial government in 1823, but it was actually a reconfirmation of an arrangement negotiated between his father and the Spanish authorities in

[31] Bradburn's certification of Benjamin R. Milam, August 12, 1824, Archivo de Fomento, Relaciones exteriores, Colonización, Archivo General de la Nación; hereafter cited as AGN; see Elizabeth H. West transcript, 308:n.p., Barker History Center, University of Texas.

1820; even so, when the empire fell, the new congress had to approve the grant.

Exactly what Col. Bradburn did between 1824 and 1828 is unknown, but in February, 1828, he sat as one of five judges at a court-martial in the Presidential Palace in Mexico City. Gen. Vicente Filisola presided, and the five absolved Col. José Codallos of guilt for an unstated charge. The case had been pending since 1826 and had been instituted by Lt. Col. Joaquín Ramírez y Sesma, acting on orders of his superior, Gen. Ignacio de Mora.[32] Bradburn, one of two colonels and three generals, would seem to have had the respect of his fellow officers to have received such an assignment.

Political events between 1824 and 1829 had not been particularly auspicious for Bradburn, but finally the Centralists wrested control from the liberal party. The first president, Guadalupe Victoria, a former revolutionary, served his four-year term without distinction. In 1828 the contest for the presidency was waged between Bradburn's former hero Vicente Guerrero, the popular candidate of the Federalist party, and Secretary of State Manuel Gómez Pedraza, a moderate. Most likely Bradburn supported Gómez Pedraza, who controlled the military vote and through questionable voting procedures defeated Guerrero. Even before his inauguration, however, the liberals staged a revolt and forced the new president to flee the country. Congress then declared that

[32] *La Águila méjicana*, May 6, 1828, trans. J. V. Clay, Wallisville Heritage Park Archives.

Guerrero was the chief executive, but at the close of 1829 the conservatives staged a coup and installed Vice-President Anastasio Bustamante as president. This unrest resulted in a military dictatorship when the Centralists, with the aid of the army, tightened control by murdering Guerrero, removing liberal governors, and placing armed guards in both Congress and the state legislatures. Bustamante's cabinet was headed by the arch-conservative secretary of state, Lucas Alamán. Mier y Terán refused an appointment as secretary of war and marine, and Bustamante made him commandant general of the Eastern Interior States, the same position Bustamante had held before December, 1829. The Eastern Interior States consisted of Coahuila-Texas and its neighbors on the southeast, Tamaulipas and Nuevo León, which strongly supported the Federalist party.[33]

Even before the political climate improved for Bradburn, he had taken advantage of his influence to secure a steamboat monopoly from the legislature of Coahuila-Texas. In the spring of 1828, Bradburn and Stephen Staples, of the commission house R. T. Staples & Company, petitioned for a fifteen-year monopoly to develop steamboat traffic on the portion of the Rio Grande that flowed through Coahuila. The boundary between Coahuila and Texas was between the Nueces and Medina rivers southwest of Béxar, and thus Coahuila controlled both banks of the Rio

[33] Fehrenback, *Fire and Blood*, pp. 366–70; Ohland Morton, "Life of General Don Manuel de Mier y Terán as It Affected Texas-Mexican Relations," *Southwestern Historical Quarterly* 47 (October, 1943–January 1944):139, 267; 48 (July–October, 1944):63–64, 193; hereafter cited as Morton, "Life of Terán."

Grande from the "big bend" down to a point about thirty miles north of Laredo. Below Laredo the river was entirely within the boundary of Tamaulipas, whose northern boundary was the Nueces River, and to travel downstream from Coahuila steamers must also have permission from Tamaulipas. The charter, granted on April 12, 1828, generously exempted the proposed undertaking from taxes, allowed the owners to cut timber from adjoining banks, gave permission for colonies on vacant land along the river, and, finally, permitted the entrepreneurs to transfer the monopoly or to delegate the powers to an agent. The project had to begin within two years, by April, 1830, or the privilege would be revoked.[34]

Bradburn was unable to activate this state charter owing to political unrest in 1828 and 1829, when election frauds and a threatened Spanish invasion occupied northeastern Mexico. He also acquired a similar license from the federal government in 1829, which was good for only six months, and he successfully petitioned Mier y Terán for an extension, but a second request to prolong the contract failed to be approved.[35]

In 1829, Bradburn made tentative arrangements with Capt. Henry Austin, a seafaring cousin of Ste-

[34] Hans P. N. Gammel, comp., *The Laws of Texas, 1822–1897*, 1:210–11.

[35] Juan Davis Bradburn to Mier y Terán, May 18, 1830, Archivo de Guerra y Marina, Operaciones militares, 1830, Fracción 1, Legajo 14, AGN: see Mattie Austin Hatcher transcript, 329:293, Barker History Center, University of Texas; hereafter cited as Guerra y Marina, Hatcher transcript.

phen F. Austin, to bring a steamboat to the Rio Grande. The captain had been in the commission business in and around Vera Cruz since 1825, and in July, 1829, he brought the shallow-draft, eighty-six-ton *Ariel* from New Orleans. Matamoros merchants, however, were suspicious about Austin's motives and his New England origins, and they failed either to invest in the undertaking or to ship sufficient goods to provide Austin with a reasonable profit. He made several trips up and down the river, even as far as Revilla, about 200 miles from the Gulf, but he found that above that point steamboat navigation was impossible because of shallow water except during the rainy season. Almost as visionary as his cousin, the captain believed that he could take advantage of the occasional high water to tap the rich fur-trapping country around Santa Fe by way of the Pecos River. He even forwarded a memorial to the State Department in Washington suggesting that the United States offer to exchange land west of the Rockies in the Louisiana Territory for Santa Fe—the United States might even offer "a couple of million dollars." Austin waited expectantly for a reply during 1829 and 1830, but he finally became discouraged in August, 1830, and took his ship from Matamoros to the Brazos, where he hoped to find enough business to make the vessel profitable. Austin's inability to ascend the river beyond Revilla may have contributed to Bradburn's lack of success in activating his charter from Coahuila-Texas, but Austin took no responsibility for the colonel's difficulty. In a letter to his cousin Austin said that his financial problems had arisen because "Bradburn has failed to perform his engagements."[36] The colonel may have lost interest in the undertaking because the political changes promised that his military career might improve.

With Bustamante in the Presidential Palace and Mier y Terán named commandant general in the northeast, an officer with no taint of federalism in his record could expect advancement. Bradburn was on leave from active duty at the end of 1829, a mere "looker-on" in Matamoros, but was expecting an appointment soon when John Joseph Linn visited him. A trader from Lavaca Bay, Linn not only traveled to Matamoros but also made the overland trip to Chihuahua. At this time Bradburn was living with his wife and son on the river road below the city, and when Mier y Terán arrived in Matamoros in March, 1830, Bradburn immediately called on him to offer his services.[37]

Mier y Terán, once a liberal reformer, had gradually moved into the Centralist party during the 1820s. Trained as an army engineer, he had developed a keen interest in natural science. Although attracted to the independence movement in 1812, he accepted royal amnesty in 1817 and spent the next five years quietly managing his family's estates. In

[36] Henry Austin to S. F. Austin, August 3, September 24, December 14, 1829; January 29, May 27, August 25, 1830; S. F. Austin to Henry Austin, August 27, 1829, *Austin Papers*, 2:244, 250–53, 259–60, 300–301, 327–28, 395–96, 473–74; *Texas Gazette*, October 24, 1829. For Henry Austin's memorial of 1829 see *Galveston News*, August 7, 1845; *Texas National Register*, August 21, 1845.

[37] "Bradburn Memorial"; John Joseph Linn, *Reminiscences of 50 Years in Texas*, p. 12.

1822 he was elected to the Constituent Congress as a conservative republican, and he served as secretary of war and marine from 1824 to 1828, during the administration of Guadalupe Victoria. In 1828 he led a scientific expedition into Texas to study the fauna and flora, determine the number and inclinations of Indian tribes and Anglo-Americans, and establish the boundary between Louisiana and Texas north of the westward bend in the Sabine River as set by the Adams-Onís Treaty in 1819. While he discovered no subversive activities among the residents of Texas, Mier y Terán remained uneasy about the intent of the government in Washington, and upon his return to Mexico City the following year he used his friendship with Secretary of State Lucas Alamán to encourage the government to limit the further emigration of Anglo-Americans into Texas. He and Alamán wanted to "Mexicanize" Texas by sending families to the frontier, and their combined effort appeared as the Law of April 6, 1830.[38]

The passage of this law provided the means for Bradburn's return to Texas. Aimed at restricting the flow of immigrants from the United States, the Law of April 6, 1830, indicated Mexico's real concern that Texas might be the next territory coveted by the United States. The statute contained a number of provisions that irritated the Anglo-Texans: incomplete colonization contracts were abrogated, further introduction of black indentured servants (a technique adopted by the Texans to avoid offending Mex-

[38] Morton, "Life of Mier y Terán," *Southwestern Historical Quarterly* 47 (October, 1943–January, 1944): 48 (July-October, 1944): 58–59.

ican sensibilities regarding slavery) was forbidden; customhouses and guards to enforce the customs laws of the nation would be placed at the various entrances to Texas upon the expiration of special exemptions from taxes that had been allowed for Austin's colonies; and Mexican and European immigration into Texas would be encouraged. The one favorable aspect of the law from the Anglo settlers' point of view was that it opened the coasting trade to foreign (American) ships; the temporary privilege was designed to divert the colonists' former dependence on New Orleans as a market by encouraging trade with Mexican ports, and since Mexican shipping was limited, foreign vessels must be allowed into the carrying trade. This easing of the traditional restrictions against foreigners participating in commerce caused great confusion when combined with imposition of tariff and tonnage duties in Texas that previously had been waived.

Clever men quickly noted the contradictory and ambiguous portions of the law and instituted formal protests. Austin maintained that his colonial endeavors included complete contracts because the state had awarded him premium land for settling a stated number of colonists even though the colonies were not entirely filled. His insistence on his privilege to introduce settlers until the original time limit was reached won grudging permission from Mier y Terán, and ship captains and merchants who complained that the tariff laws were unclear secured a temporary reprieve from paying duty.

Mier y Terán immediately recognized that Bradburn possessed excellent qualifications for commanding the proposed new post on Galveston Bay, which was the best harbor on the Texas coast and was situated near the center of the Anglo community. Because Bradburn was bilingual and had acceptable political connections, Mier y Terán transferred him immediately to his command. On April 18, only twelve days after the passage of the Law of April 6, Mier y Terán arranged for issuance of a two-month passport to Bradburn so that he might visit New Orleans to buy a boat and also gauge the military strength of the United States along the Sabine River.[39]

Bradburn left on May 18, spent only a few days in New Orleans, and then toured western Louisiana, where he discovered that garrisons had been strengthened ostensibly to control smuggling. He found no indication that the United States planned any overt action against Mexican Texas. On his return he visited Austin's colony, where he found that most settlers were law-abiding and that the few troublemakers could be controlled by the empresario if he was given proper support. He returned to Matamoros in June and planned to make a quick trip to explore Galveston Bay aboard one of the government schooners, but it appears doubtful that he made the voyage.[40]

On October 4, 1830, Mier y Terán issued formal

[39] Ibid., 48 (July–October, 1944): 54, 173; Order from Mier y Terán, April 15, 1830, Instructions, Manuel Yturria to Juan Davis Bradburn, May 18, 1830, Guerra y Marina, Hatcher transcript, 329:295.

[40] Henry Austin to S. F. Austin, July 2, 1830, Austin Papers, 2:435–37; Juan Davis Bradburn to Mier y Terán, June 12, 1830, Guerra y Marina, Hatcher transcript, 329:281.

orders to Bradburn with a flattering cover letter praising him for his zeal in working for the prosperity of Mexico. As Bradburn's reward, Mier y Terán was giving him command of a detachment to establish a town and fort on Galveston Bay. The orders explained that the post was being created in response to the Law of April 6, 1830. A copy of the statute was included with the orders. There followed nineteen paragraphs of instructions to Bradburn on the selection of the site; the attitude he should assume toward the Anglo settlers in the nearby Atascosito community, about twenty-one miles from the mouth of the Trinity River, including encouraging the use of the Spanish language and assuring the colonists that the national government intended the new military settlement to protect them and to promote prosperity for all; construction of the garrison and the supporting town; administration of the command and his relationship with the military officers at Nacogdoches and Béxar; the course to follow when making contact with the Alabama Coushatta Indian villages north of the Atascosito community; and, finally, exploration of the land between the Trinity and the Sabine to determine whether steamboat transportation was possible on those rivers. Mier y Terán concluded his instructions by promising military advancement for Bradburn and his officers if the plan was efficiently and successfully executed.[41]

---

[41] Mier y Terán's instructions to Bradburn, October 4, 1830, Spanish Archives, General Land Office of Texas, 53:141–45; hereafter cited as Mier y Terán to Bradburn, October 4, 1830. A copy of these instructions also appears in Guerra y Marina, Hatcher transcript, 329:267–75.

Bradburn and his men left Matamoros in October aboard the United States merchant sloop *Alabama Packet* bound for Galveston Bay. The captain, Perkins Lovejoy, of New Orleans, had been one of the first to take advantage of the opening of the Mexican coasting trade to foreigners. He had sailed for Harrisburg, on Buffalo Bayou, which emptied into the San Jacinto estuary that formed an arm of upper Galveston Bay. He had discharged twenty-five passengers and a cargo of wheat and tobacco in July and one month later had loaded lumber and hides for Matamoros. The fifty-two-foot, thirty-ton vessel drew only four feet of water, which permitted it to cross Red Fish Reef, the oystershell barrier halfway up Galveston Bay that prevented larger ships from ascending to the settlements. Bradburn, officers, and men crowded the small American vessel, while their baggage and supplies followed in a schooner of Mexican registry.[42]

The three officers who accompanied Bradburn were Lts. Ignacio Domínguez, Juan M. Pacho, and José Rincón. Mier y Terán had named Domínguez adjutant and Pacho paymaster, and the pair shared the command of thirteen regulars from the Company of Pueblo Viejo who had seen service during the recent Spanish attack and who were also specially chosen for this enterprise because they were fishermen and oarsmen, possessing skills necessary for survival in Gal-

[42] Morton, "Life of Mier y Terán," *Southwestern Historical Quarterly* 47 (October, 1943–January, 1944):505; "Bradburn Memorial"; W. D. Dunlap to George Fisher, July 21, 1830, in George Fisher to S. M. Williams, July 27, 1830, Williams Papers; *Texas Gazette*, July 3, 1830; Works Projects Administration (WPA), *Ship Registers and Enrollments of New Orleans, Louisiana, 1821–1830*, 2:3–4.

veston Bay. Rincón commanded twenty new recruits from the Twelfth Permanent Battalion and also six convict soldiers who were to perform the heavy labor of felling trees and building roads at the frontier post. The former prisoners had been released to the military when they volunteered for service in Texas. Their crimes varied from serious to trivial.[43] Rumors about the convicts assigned to Texas frightened the Anglo-American residents, and their number and the expected atrocities were magnified with each repetition.

The *Alabama Packet* reached Perry's Point, on upper Galveston Bay, on October 26 after a stormy passage. The schooner carrying the supplies had gone down, and in spite of salvage efforts the staple provisions had been soaked and had to be discarded.[44]

The thirty-foot bluff commanded the marshy entrance to the Trinity River. Although several channels cut through the sandy delta, the deepest followed the eastern bank under the bluff. Even so, the sloop had to anchor a short distance offshore, and the men had to wade ashore or wait turns for places in the ship's rowboat to reach the wide beach below the steep bank. The strategic site had not changed much in the fourteen years since Bradburn and Perry had camped there. Driftwood and clumps of trees lined

[43] "Bradburn Memorial"; Mier y Terán to Bradburn, October 4, 1830; Alejandro Yhary, Captain of the Port, November 18, 1830, Guerra y Marina, Hatcher transcript, 329:265–66. Yhary says that one of the seven convicts escaped.

[44] Juan Davis Bradburn to Antonio Elosúa, November 4, 1830, Béxar Archives, Barker History Center, University of Texas at Austin, roll 135, frame 0980.

the beach, and after climbing up the cliff, the men found themselves on a pleasantly wooded plain that sloped eastward to the open prairie. An old Indian trail ran north along the top of the bluff and skirted Turtle Bayou, just northeast of the mouth of the river, and continued about twenty-five miles to the Atascosito crossing of the Coushatta Road from La Bahía to Opelousas. Mier y Terán relied on Bradburn's memory in choosing the inland location; his orders forbade Bradburn to subject the force to exposure on the coastal islands or peninsula. Only a hut would be constructed there for the guards who would monitor vessels entering and leaving the bay.[45]

From the beginning Bradburn was plagued with a number of frustrating circumstances over which he had little control. First he had to replace the lost stores, but an unusually dry season provided little surplus corn in the neighborhood. On November 26 he sent the schooner *Galveston*, evidently purchased on his earlier trip to New Orleans, to the Crescent City for provisions. December brought cold rain, and his troops were ill-prepared for the Texas northers; lacking proper winter clothing, those unfortunates who were temporarily assigned duty on Galveston Island suffered terribly from exposure. Moreover, Mier y Terán failed to realize, and Bradburn had apparently forgotten, how little farming could be done during the rainy winter months. Plans to plant corn, beans, and sweet potatoes to sustain the garrison during the following year were delayed because of the

[45] Mier y Terán to Bradburn, October 4, 1830; Anonymous, *A Visit to Texas in 1831*, p. 60.

rain and wind and also because of the scarcity of oxen, mules, or horses to plow the land. Mier y Terán had added extra money to the budget earmarked for hiring or buying draft animals from the Anglo farmers, but Bradburn discovered that few were available. Instead, the convict troops and the few recruits who did not yet have "the military habit of resisting another occupation than that of service" put in a small garden. Mier y Terán's long-range plan encouraged each soldier to farm a small plot of land that could become his own at the end of his enlistment, and a few considered the offer. By this means Mier y Terán hoped eventually to establish a strong Mexican colony.[46]

In March, 1831, Col. Bradburn reported that he had laid out the new town of Anahuac, a military village with a few civilian merchants and artisans lured away from Atascosito. By the National Colonization Act of 1824, which was part of the federal constitution, the states had been awarded control over their own territory in the matter of colonization, but the national government reserved the right to appropriate vacant land for military purposes and to settle families who did not apply to one of the empresarios holding state contracts. Thus the village of Anahuac derived its authority from the federal government through the local military commander, unlike civilian towns, which were subject to the civil laws of the state.

[46] Mier y Terán to Bradburn, October 4, 1830; J. D. Bradburn to Mier y Terán, November 22, 1830, January 24, March 4, 1831, Wagner Collection.

Not all Anglo-American settlers comprehended the difference, a situation that caused Bradburn's subsequent actions to be widely misunderstood.

The colonel made a map of his new village for Mier y Terán, calling the commandant general's attention to the patriotic naming of the streets after the states in the Mexican federation. A visitor to Anahuac in March, 1831, reported that the village contained fifteen or twenty houses and seven stores, and in a letter to Mier y Terán at about the same time Bradburn remarked that more warehouses were needed in which to store the goods that were arriving regularly at the port.[47]

A merchant who arrived at Anahuac in March confirmed Bradburn's rosy picture of commercial activities on Galveston Bay. The merchant, Nicholas D. Labadie, was also a doctor and ministered to both the civilian population and the troops. In only sixteen days he had recorded $115 on his medical charge book and was seeing at least six patients a day. In a letter to a nephew Labadie urged him to move to Texas, where he could expect a profit of 50 to 100 percent on groceries—whiskey was selling for seventy-five cents a gallon, and flour for twelve dollars a barrel. The garrison was paid regularly, and each soldier also received twenty-five cents a day for food and drink. There were 170 troops and more due to arrive,

---

[47] Bradburn to Mier y Terán, March 4, 1831, Wagner Collection; Anonymous, *A Visit to Texas in 1831*, p. 60. Anahuac had been named before January, 1831; see Tomás Oquilla to Antonio Elosúa, January 29, 1831, Béxar Archives, roll 138, frame 0333.

while the civilian population had reached 300 in June, and more European immigrants were expected through the auspices of the New York–based Galveston Bay and Texas Land Company. Labadie warned his nephew that small change and lumber were very scarce but that if he wanted to build with brick, Bradburn's two kilns produced brick that the colonel sold for five dollars a thousand. No duties were levied on goods at that time, only tonnage, but a customhouse had been erected on Galveston island.[48]

The fort did not progress as rapidly as the village did. The troops first erected a temporary wooden barracks, presumably by placing saplings vertically in a shallow earth trench, the typical building technique of northern Mexico. The upright poles, usually 6 feet long, were placed as close together as possible and snugly laced with leather thongs or grass plaits. A thatched roof completed the building, and the walls could be plastered with clay to keep out the cold. The only description of the structure, provided by an unnamed visitor in 1831, noted its overall dimensions— 150 feet long and 20 feet wide—but said nothing about its appearance except that Bradburn's quarters were in one end and the guardhouse in the other. The visitor also recorded a few details that provide a glimpse of everyday life at the barracks. Many of the men kept hunting dogs, which on one occasion treed Bradburn's pet cat. Hunting was a major diversion for the officers and the men of the village, and Bradburn was among the foremost aficionados of the

[48] Nicholas Labadie to Anthony Lagrave, February 13, March 19, June 14, 1831, Nicholas Labadie Papers, Rosenberg Library, Galveston.

sport. The men had captured a bear and kept it tied to a tree, but for what purpose was not recorded.[49]

The permanent fort was to be made of brick, according to a cardboard plan Mier y Terán gave Bradburn, and the commandant budgeted $2,000 for its construction. The convict soldiers were to do the heavy construction work, assisted by the other troops, and if no brickmakers were to be found among the troops, Bradburn could hire local artisans. Clay deposits were available nearby, and the oystershell middens that dotted the coast could supply the lime. By March the brick kilns were being readied.

Two months later the foundation was complete, and Bradburn organized a celebration to commemorate the laying of the cornerstone. He invited the nearby Atascosito community in an effort to repair the strained relations that had developed between the Anglos and him over land matters, and, according to his report to Mier y Terán, a number of people attended the day-long festivities on May 14. Lt. Pacho, in Masonic regalia and representing the honorary but absent sponsor, Col. José Mariano Guerra, of Tamaulipas, laid the first stone with the help of Bradburn, also a Mason, and the alcalde (mayor) of Anahuac, William Hardin. After the stone was set, the crowd moved to a shaded area, where a color guard presented the flags accompanied by fife and drum and followed by three volleys from the cannons. Hardin then delivered an oration, presumably in Spanish, in keeping with Mier y Terán's directive, and when the

[49] Mier y Terán to Bradburn, October 4, 1830; Anonymous, *A Visit to Texas in 1831*, pp. 60, 63, 80.

ceremony was over, the guests enjoyed a banquet provided by the local merchants. Bradburn offered a toast to the success of the new town and the support it was receiving from the government, and Pacho raised his glass to the "undying memory" of the commandant general. The celebration continued until dusk, when the guests returned to their homes.

Work continued on the fort through the summer and fall, and supervision of the construction passed from the overburdened Pacho to new officers who had arrived with reinforcements sent by Mier y Terán. Bradburn, now forty-four years old and particular about details, was not satisfied with parts of the fort, and he ordered some of the work redone on one of the gun emplacements. The directive angered one junior officer, who henceforth was Bradburn's enemy.[50]

Bradburn's troubles with the Anglo-American residents began when José Francisco Madero, the state-appointed land commissioner, arrived in January, 1831, to issue titles to those living east of the San Jacinto River, beyond Austin's empresario grant. The confrontation between the two men was both personal and political and revolved around each one's concept of centralism and federalism, the issue that had divided the nation for a decade. Bradburn, the Centralist military commander of Galveston Bay, took a particularly narrow nationalistic view of his powers

[50] Mier y Terán to Bradburn, October 4, 1830; Juan Davis Bradburn to Antonio Elosúa, May 14, 1831, Béxar Archives, roll 141, frame 0141, translated typescript copy in Wallisville Heritage Park Archives.

and that of the central government when challenged by a proponent of states' rights. Madero, a native of Coahuila, a civilian, and a member of the Federalist party, owed his appointment to the Federalist governor of Coahuila-Texas and was charged by state law to give titles to those residents of eastern Texas who lived outside the authority of any empresario grants or *ayuntamientos* (town councils) and who were in residence before 1828. The immediate quarrel was twofold: (1) could the state issue titles when Article 11 of the Law of April 6, 1830, abrogated pending incomplete contracts and forbade Anglo-Americans from becoming citizens of Texas; and (2) could the state give legal possession to those of foreign birth living in the border and coastal reserve? To protect Mexican borders and coastline from aggressive filibusterers, the national constitution of 1824 had barred nonnatives from living within twenty-six miles of the Gulf and fifty-two miles of the Sabine River. Despite this restriction the state government had allowed Anglos to settle along the coast in Austin's first colony, thereby setting a precedent. Moreover, many of those still waiting for titles in 1831 had settled along Galveston Bay and the Sabine before 1824 and thus claimed retroactive rights.

Madero arrived in San Felipe, the capital of Austin's colony, early in January and on January 15 published a notice in the *Texas Gazette* that he would soon be in the Atascosito neighborhood to complete surveys and issue titles. His commission from the state government represented a long-awaited promise to give legal posssession to those who had settled beyond any recognized jurisdiction. In 1828 both national and state authorities had agreed that the settlers deserved titles, and the state had dispatched a commissioner the following year. But upon his arrival in Nacogdoches early in 1830, he had been arrested on a contrived charge apparently to prevent him from carrying out his commission. By the end of the year it appeared that the first commissioner would remain incarcerated indefinitely, and the state named Madero to succeed him. Avoiding Nacogdoches for obvious reasons, Madero determined to begin on the Trinity and later move northeast.[51]

When Madero arrived at Atascosito, he failed to make the usual courtesy call on the ranking military commander of that district, an omisson that indicated his scorn for Bradburn. Madero was a friend of the deposed President Guerrero, which put him at odds with the military commander on Galveston Bay. As a member of the first state legislature in 1828, Madero had been one of the three deputies who signed Bradburn's steamboat privilege, and perhaps there was animosity over the failure to carry out a project that would have enhanced the well-being of the state. In any event, Bradburn learned about the commissioner's intentions not through an interview but by reading the notice in the *Gazette*. Schooled in military protocol, Bradburn viewed Madero's disregard for the proprieties as both a slight to the national government and disrespect for his position. Rereading his instructions and his copy of the Law of April 6, he

<hr />

[51] *Texas Gazette*, Janaury 15, 1831.

decided that Madero was violating the law. On January 24 he wrote to Mier y Terán asking for advice: "Your Excellency will kindly let me know as soon as possible what I should do, since I find myself obligated by orders I have here to tell him that his commission violates the Law of April. 6."[52]

The following day Bradburn sent Madero a warning that his plan was prohibited both by Article 11 of the Law of April 6, which in Bradburn's view abrogated the 1828 contract to issue titles, and by the 1824 national colonization act, which proscribed foreigners from living in the coastal reserve. The Atascosito community, not even a village but an aggregate of farms lining the Trinity River near the old crossing on the Coushatta Road, was within the ten-league (twenty-six-mile) littoral reserve if measured from Trinity Bay. Bradburn added that he was acting on orders from Mier y Terán, a statement that cannot be proved by extant orders. The October 4 instructions from Mier y Terán to Bradburn directed the colonel to reassure the Atascosito residents that their titles would be forthcoming, though the next, somewhat ambiguous sentence urged Bradburn to offer settlers titles from the national government as an alternative. A later paragraph confirmed that residents who had arrived before April 6, 1830, could become citizens and hold land but that all subsequent immigrants had to apply to the national government for permission to settle. It is entirely possible, of course, that Mier y

[52] Juan Davis Bradburn to Mier y Terán, January 24, 1831, Wagner Collection; S. F. Austin to S. M. Williams, December 28, 1830, Williams Papers.

Terán later gave Bradburn oral instructions to follow a narrower construction of the laws and, in fact, the commandant general did support Bradburn's interpretation when it was challenged by Madero.[53]

Bradburn's narrow view that he, as the representative of the supreme government, had sole authority to issue titles or to order surveys in all cases in which individuals had located in the littoral reserve or had arrived after April 6, 1830, aroused hostility among the Anglo-Americans. They felt that his dictum was arrogant and capricious and characteristic of the hated Bustamante military regime; like their contemporaries in the United States, the settlers believed that states' rights should take precedence in the matter.

For his part Madero denied that his commission violated national law and said that he planned to observe carefully the provisions of Article 11. This answer failed to satisfy the colonel, and on January 29 he invited the land commissioner to meet with him at Anahuac. Madero refused, reluctant to appear subservient to the Centralist regime. By this time the community was aroused against Bradburn's presumed usurpation of civilian rights. Anglos began comparing Bradburn and the Centralist party with King George III, who in their view had persecuted freedom-loving republicans. Protest meetings were held, and the settlers wrongly concluded that Mexico City had determined to deny them state-issued titles

[53] Juan Davis Bradburn to J. F. Madero, January 25, 1831; Mier y Terán to Antonio Elosúa, March 26, 1831, Spanish Archives, General Land Office, 44:21, 30; Mier y Terán to Bradburn, October 4, 1830; "Bradburn Memorial."

and that they would be forced to apply to Bradburn for land.

Bradburn and Madero kept up their arguments in a steady stream of letters; the colonel insisted that all contracts had been annulled, and Madero rebutted that such an interpretation gave the law an "*ex post facto* effect." Rumors reached Anahuac that the settlers planned an assault on the small, unfinished garrison, and Bradburn decided to take the offensive. He led a small contingent to Atascosito, where he forced an interview with Madero on February 12. They agreed to suspend their activities until they could receive word from their superiors, but after Madero returned to his supporters, he sent word back that he needed time to consider such action. Bradburn gave him until 9:00 the next morning, February 13. When the land commissioner failed to appear, Bradburn ordered his arrest and that of his assistant, José María Carbajal. A fellow Federalist with markedly republican notions, Carbajal, a native of Béxar, had been educated in the United States and had returned just in time to act as Madero's interpreter and surveyor. Because Atascosito lacked facilities to hold the prisoners, Bradburn marched them to Anahuac and prepared to defend his position from a rumored attack.[54] Calmer heads prevailed, and loose talk about an armed march against Anahuac faded when John A. Williams, a long-term resident of eastern Texas and reputedly one of the leaders of the

[54] Bradburn-Madero correspondence, January 25–February 6, 1831, Spanish Archives, General Land Office, 44:21–27; "Bradburn Memorial."

movement against Bradburn, denied that any such attack had been planned.

The confrontation between the two stubborn men, Bradburn and Madero, produced a flurry of letters between their civil and military superiors. The political chief in Béxar—really a subgovernor for Texas—received word of Madero's arrest on February 17, four days after the event. He immediately complained to Bradburn's designated local superior, Col. Antonio Elosúa, commandant of the Béxar District, and asked him to order Bradburn to refrain from interfering with the acts of a state official. The *jefe* hoped that Elosúa's orders would be issued "in a positive manner" that would "leave no room for arbitrary interpretations."[55] When Mier y Terán received Bradburn's appeal of January 25, he asked governor José María Viesca, who was about to leave office as executive of Coahuila-Texas, to cancel Madero's powers in cases where the land involved was within the coastal or border reserve, which, of course, the governor refused to do. The commandant general then suggested to Secretary of State Alamán that, while the settlers deserved titles, the documents should come from the national commissioner, not a state representative.[56]

[55] John A. Williams to J. Davis Bradburn, February 28, 1831, Nacogdoches Archives, Blake Collection, 12:232–33; Ramón Músquiz to Antonio Elosúa, February 27, 1831, Wagner Collection, trans. Probert, Wallisville Heritage Park Archives. See also letters to and from the various officials, February 11 to 28, 1831, in Spanish Archives, General Land Office, 44:27–38.

[56] Mier y Terán to Alamán, February 9, 21, 28, 1831; J. M. Viesca to Mier y Terán, February 19, 1831, paraphrased in Morton, "Life of Mier y Terán," *Southwestern Historical Quarterly* 48 (July–October, 1944):506.

While the higher officials ruminated over the course to pursue through the sticky prerogatives of state versus nation, Bradburn pursued his investigation of the rumored insurrection. Madero's arrest had frightened the alcalde of Atascosito, and he resigned and departed from the neighborhood, which left the community without a civil government. John A. Williams appealed to the political *jefe* at Béxar for remedy, because in his view Bradburn was exerting excessive military pressure on him and the others supposedly involved with the alleged plan to attack Anahuac.[57]

Bradburn received orders to release Madero and Carbajal within ten days of their arrest, and during March and early April the pair worked diligently to complete the surveys and issue deeds before further orders interrupted their task. A crew of Anglo surveyors, including George W. Smyth, Bartlett Sims, Benjamin Tennille, and Samuel C. Hirams, had been working on some of the surveys since early spring of the previous year under the direction of the former commissioner, and within six weeks their field notes were ready to accompany the titles. Madero issued two deeds on March 2, but the rest of the sixty documents were dated between April 23 and May 12. Most were for the Atascosito residents, though a few were for sites on the Neches River, and several were large tracts located for native Mexican speculators holding eleven league certificates.[58]

[57]John A. Williams to Political Chief, March 22, 1831, Nacogdoches Archives, Blake Collection, 12:242–46.

[58]Titles issued by Madero abstracted from Virginia H. Taylor, *The*

Because of the continued friction between Bradburn and Madero the political chief finally ordered the commissioner to suspend his activities until a complete investigation by both state and federal authorities could be made. The order, dated April 2, arrived on the Trinity on the twelfth, but Madero hastened to finish documents for land already surveyed. On April 14 the *jefe* asked Madero to name a substitute commissioner who could proceed to Nacogdoches and issue titles, and the busy official named his friend José Antonio Navarro, of Béxar, who was approved by the end of the month.[59]

Madero's most controversial act, and a direct challenge to Bradburn, was the establishment of an *ayuntamiento* for the Atascosito neighborhood. The creation of the council was a function of the state, and Madero clearly had the authority under his commission, but placing it within the littoral was a direct affront to the supreme government. He installed the popularly elected body on May 2 and formally named the community Villa de la Santissima Trinidad de la Libertad, shortened to Liberty by the Anglo residents. The symbolic name was perhaps selected by the community, many of whom came from villages of that name in the United States; they selected the site from two possible locations along the Trinity, prefer-

---

Spanish Archives of the General Land Office of Texas, pp. 151–258; Barker, *Life of Austin*, p. 326, says that Madero ceased issuing titles, an error followed by subsequent writers until Miriam Partlow, *Liberty, Liberty County, and Atascosito District*, p. 77.

[59] Madero to Músquiz, April 14, 1831; José Antonio Navarro to Músquiz, April 26, 1831; Músquiz to Madero, May 1, 1832; Músquiz to Navarro, May 8, 1831, Spanish Archives, General Land Office, 44:9–15.

ring the one farthest from Bradburn's military post and close to the old Indian trail and smuggling road from Opelousas, Louisiana, to La Bahía.[60] The installation of a rival town near Anahuac angered Bradburn, who, of course, denied its legality, though for the present he suffered its existence. Less than two weeks after Liberty was created, Bradburn organized a celebration at Anahuac to commemorate laying the cornerstone of the fort, a somewhat obvious undertaking intended to diminish the importance of Liberty. Although Madero was still at Liberty, one assumes that he did not attend the festivities on May 13 but instead left for Béxar, which he reached on June 6. He then returned to his home near the Rio Grande, where he finished work on papers connected with the Liberty community.[61]

Bradburn had a number of other pressing concerns besides Madero. The men of the cavalry company sent from La Bahía to strengthen his garrison became restless when their pay failed to arrive, and a number of them deserted, as did five members of the Twelfth Battalion. Desertions plagued other Mexican commanders in Texas, so the defections cannot be blamed entirely on the situation at Anahuac. A great deal of the trouble rested in the problem of building a fort on the frontier, and later the colonel complained that his officers came to hate him because he made

[60] Partlow, *Liberty*, pp. 79–82; Liberty Ayuntamiento to Béxar Ayuntamiento, May 5, 1831, Béxar Archives, roll 140, frame 0885.

[61] Letters to and from Madero, June 6–August 12, 1831, Spanish Archives, General Land Office, 44:61–63, 69–71, 79, 83; J. F. Madero to S. M. Williams, July 15, 1831, Williams Papers.

them work so hard at nonmilitary tasks in the "wilderness."[62]

Another cause for concern was the number of impoverished European immigrants who arrived at Anahuac expecting to find housing on the former Vehlein grant, which surrounded the eastern edge of Galveston Bay and which had been annulled by the Law of April 6. Joseph Vehlein, Lorenzo de Zavala, and David G. Burnet had secured empresario contracts from the state in 1827 encompassing eastern Texas from the Trinity River watershed to the Sabine and extending north above the Old Spanish Road near Nacogdoches. Nothing been done with the contracts before 1830 and the trio had sold their rights to a group of New York speculators who organized the Galveston Bay and Texas Land Company. Both the sale and the speculative foreign venture violated national and state laws, but nevertheless, the New Yorkers dispatched a number of settlers in 1831, believing that any obstacles could be overcome by the influential agents they expected to employ. The unwary colonists bought land scrip from the company, believing that they had purchased a number of acres in Texas. Bradburn was sympathetic with their plight and endeavored to provide temporary plots within his military community.[63] The colonel felt sorry for the set-

[62] Bradburn to Mier y Terán, March 4, 1831, Wagner Collection; for desertions see Antonio Elosúa to Severo Ruíz, October 12, 1830; Francisco Ruíz to Antonio Elosúa, January 7, 1831; Antonio Elosúa to Major, January 10, 1831, McLean, ed. and comp., *Papers Concerning Robertson's Colony in Texas*, 5:74, 393, 401; "Bradburn Memorial."

[63] J. D. Bradburn to S. M. Williams, March 31, 1831, Williams Papers.

tlers who had been cheated by the investors and had been led into the predicament in part because of the illegal activities of his old adversary Lorenzo de Zavala, an ardent Federalist.

An additional aggravation was overseeing the collection of port duties and controlling the smuggling of goods through the Anglo community and into the interior of northern Mexico. The various temporary exemptions from tariff duties granted to Austin's colonists in the 1820s had set a precedent, and few understood that the time limit had expired. The dichotomy created by the Law of April 6, 1830, in opening the coasting trade to foreign vessels while at the same time providing for the collection of customs duties further clouded the issue for collectors, merchants, and ship captains. The merchants and ship captains continued to demand the previous exemptions because of poor communication, poorly written or translated laws, and an instinctive dislike and suspicion of Mexican collectors.

Soon after Bradburn arrived on Galveston Bay, S. Rhoads Fisher, formerly of Pennsylvania, brought his sixty-five-ton schooner, *Champion*, into the bay. He had left New Orleans with a cargo bound for Copano Bay, the port used by residents of Béxar and La Bahía but had left there in ballast seeking a return cargo. He had paid tonnage duties at his first port of call, had then sailed into Matagorda Bay but had found nothing to load, and had traveled on to Galveston Bay, where he had contracted to take a load of lumber from the steam sawmill at Harrisburg to Tampico. He discovered to his dismay in talking with Bradburn that he would have to pay tonnage at Galveston and again at Tampico because of the way the law was written. Bradburn listened sympathetically to Fisher's complaints and agreed that such overcharging would drive foreign captains out of the coasting tradé. He promised to take up the matter with Mier y Terán. Fisher wrote Stephen F. Austin that he found the colonel a "gentleman" just as the empresario had said, which indicates that as late as January, 1831, Austin had found no fault with Bradburn. Fisher's overcharges were later refunded, and Mier y Terán made suitable adjustments to continue to encourage foreign coasting captains to visit Mexican ports.[64]

The residents of Harrisburg disliked the monitoring of their activities by the nearby military establishment. One of Madero's surveyors, Samuel Hirams, who had his own reasons for disliking the colonel, advised Fisher to ignore orders from Anahuac because Bradburn's jurisdiction did not include Austin's colony. Whether his statement was merely malicious, reflected what Hirams had heard from Madero, or was the common opinion of the Anglo community is unknown, but such advice made Bradburn's role difficult. To counter this kind of prejudice, Bradburn wrote to Samuel May Williams, Austin's lieutenant in San Felipe, for assistance. Williams was in charge of colonial affairs during the empresario's absence; Austin was in Saltillo, where he was serving as an elected deputy in the legislative session in prog-

[64] S. Rhoads Fisher to S. F. Austin, January 10, 1831; Terán to S. F. Austin, March 21, 1831, *Austin Papers*, 2:583–84, 622–23; S. F. Austin to S. M. Williams, April 16, 1831, Williams Papers.

ress. Williams suggested naming John Austin or some other respected member of the Anglo community to administer the collection of tonnage on the Brazos and even naming someone at Harrisburg for the same purpose. Bradburn probably knew John Austin from the days of the empire, when Austin had accompanied Ben Milam and Félix Trespalacios to the capital. Following Williams's advice, the colonel approached Austin, but he refused and suggested William Dobie Dunlap, a merchant of Anahuac and Harrisburg. Dunlap had served only a few weeks when the antipathy of his fellow Americans forced him to resign. John Austin asked for the position of captain of the port at the Brazos. Bradburn granted the request and named James Lindsay to act as collector. These interim appointments cooled the discontent brewing along the Brazos, mainly because neither Lindsay nor Austin rigidly enforced the law and collected only minimal fees.[65]

Mier y Terán, however, was under pressure from the supreme government to establish the customhouse on Galveston Bay as provided by law, and after eighteen months of procrastination he finally decided to act. Although collecting tonnage on visiting vessels brought in a little money, it was not sufficient revenue for government needs. Neither the states nor the nation taxed land or wealth; both depended on excise taxes for their revenue, a traditional form of taxation

[65]"Bradburn Memorial"; J. D. Bradburn to Mier y Terán, March 4, 1831, Wagner Collection; S. M. Williams to W. D. Dunlap, March 9, 10, 1831; S. M. Williams to John Austin [March 20, 1831?], *Austin Papers*, 2:609–10, 621; J. D. Bradburn to S. M. Williams, March 31, 1831, Williams Papers.

inherited from Spain. Because the Anglo-Texans evinced so much hostility over relinquishing the previous tariff exemptions, the government deviated from enforcing the uniform duties of Mexico and allowed the Texans the privilege of importing all necessary provisions duty-free but retaining the collection of tonnage, the levy on tobacco, and certain other specified items at the ports of Matagorda and Galveston. In September, 1831, Mier y Terán named George Fisher collector of the port of Galveston.

Fisher had tried to open the customhouse in Texas in May, 1830, using a commission probably issued by his friend Lorenzo de Zavala, secretary of the treasury during the brief Guerrero administration in 1829. A native of Hungary, Fisher immigrated to the United States in 1815 at the age of twenty and settled near Vicksburg, Mississippi. In 1825 he journeyed to Mexico City, where he became an associate of the United States chargé d'affaires, Joel R. Poinsett, and he took an active part in establishing the politically liberal York Rite Masonic movement. A confirmed republican and a member of the Federalist faction, Fisher had to flee from Mexico in 1830, when Bustamante took over the government. Ever an opportunist, Fisher decided to activate his unused commision as a means of support after the Law of April 6 opened the ports to foreign commerce and the tariff exemptions had expired. He presented himself to Stephen F. Austin in San Felipe in May, 1830, and the two agreed that Fisher should temporarily open the *aduana* (customhouse) at the mouth of the Brazos

River, where most of the vessels called, pending approval from Mier y Terán. For six weeks Fisher busily issued orders, posted notices, and seized contraband tobacco, but on July 1 he received orders from the commandant general to suspend his operation because, Mier y Terán said, opening the coasting trade to foreign ships made the customhouse unnecessary.[66]

The real reason for Fisher's suspension was political: he was a Federalist appointee, and Mier y Terán was unsure about what course to follow until he could consult with Alamán. In the interim Fisher found a position as bilingual secretary to the San Felipe *ayuntamiento*, a job that lasted only until October, when the council decided that he was a spy for Mier y Terán and dismissed him. The unlucky man returned to Matamoros, Mier y Terán's headquarters, and worked his way into the general's confidence. On September 27, 1831, Fisher received orders to open the *aduana* on Bolivar Peninsula and a branch office on the Brazos to control the smuggling of goods into the interior. Mier y Terán named Lt. Juan Pacho, Bradburn's commissary, to serve as Fisher's assistant and promised him a regular guard that would come from posts with surplus troops. Fisher appointed Francisco Mansue y Duclor as deputy on the Brazos, but the new deputy collector was unable to leave his post as clerk in the Matamoros customhouse until the end of the year. Although Fisher had expected to embark

[66]Bessie Lucille Letts, "George Fisher" (M.A. thesis, University of Texas, 1928), pp. 27, 29, 33, 35–36; Mier y Terán to George Fisher, May 24, 1830, *Austin Papers*, 2:394–95.

immediately, his journey was delayed until November because Mier y Terán decided to accompany him and personally establish the Galveston *aduana*.[67]

The party arrived at Anahuac on November 9 and during the first week toured the district, meeting with the residents. In spite of efforts to woo Mier y Terán with speeches and dinners, the commandant general did not like what he saw and determined to increase the influence of the supreme government over the neighborhood to diminish the Anglo-Americanization of the vicinity. The lack of respect for Mexican law disturbed him, and his subsequent orders were designed to tighten control over the foreign element in Texas, somewhat like a patriarch disciplining his rebellious family.

In the matter of the *aduana*, Mier y Terán approved of Fisher's plan to lease two buildings at Anahuac for a temporary office and warehouse until suitable buildings could be erected on Bolivar Peninsula and at the mouth of the Brazos. While the guard was supposedly en route, it was not known when they might arrive, and a detachment of twenty men was ordered from Anahuac to the mouth of the Brazos. Bradburn's temporary appointees, John Austin and James Lindsay, were to submit their funds and reports to Fisher immediately, but until Duclor arrived, the Brazos lacked a collector. Neither the deputy collector nor the guard had arrived by November 24, when Mier y Terán was ready to leave, and apparently as an emergency measure the commandant gen-

[67] Letts, "George Fisher," pp. 59–60, 75–77.

eral gave Fisher instructions to oversee the collections himself, evidently without any specific instructions. Mier y Terán later denounced Fisher's subsequent order of November 24 as impolitic, though the collector insisted that the general had himself issued it. Fisher's impractical order instructed all ship captains and merchants to clear their papers at Anahuac, a distance of over one hundred miles as the crow flies and many more by water through Galveston Bay or by land, skirting the marshy terrain around the San Jacinto and Trinity estuaries. The language of the directive did not suggest that the order was only a temporary measure for a matter of a few weeks until the deputy collector arrived. The Anglo residents along the lower Brazos assumed that Fisher was merely exercising his power over them as a means of revenge for their treatment of him the previous year.[68]

Mier y Terán's orders to Bradburn proved just as controversial as those to Fisher. The creation of Liberty particularly annoyed the commandant general, and he issued instructions to Bradburn designed to destroy the rival community in favor of Anahuac as the seat of government. First he ordered Bradburn to direct all the settlers residing in either the coastal or the border reserve to present their permits to do so from the central government for inspection in accordance with the national colonization law of August 18, 1824. If any resident lacked such a document, he could apply for one through Bradburn. Furthermore, all settlers had to show the colonel their titles or

[68] Ibid., pp. 83–84; Morton, "Life of Mier y Terán," *Southwestern Historical Quarterly* 48 (July–October, 1944):512–13.

the concessions that they had received from the state commissioner.[69]

A second concern was the number of men in Liberty professing to be lawyers; to Mier y Terán they appeared like a "plague of locusts" and they seemed to be idlers and troublemakers. To weed out the "cornstalk" lawyers (a frontier term for those without credentials), he ordered that all those practicing law before the *ayuntamiento* in Liberty first had to present their licenses to Bradburn. Among the lawyers practicing in Liberty were William B. Travis and Patrick Churchill Jack. Both men had trained in the United States by working with established laywers until they were sufficiently prepared to pass county bar examinations. Whether such a county license satisfied Bradburn is unclear. Mexican lawyers had to obtain a license at the state capital; as far as can be determined, Thomas Jefferson Chambers was the only Anglo lawyer in Liberty who had such a certificate.

A native of South Carolina, Travis had become a lawyer in Monroe County, Alabama, in the late 1820s and, at about age twenty-one, had arrived in Texas in May, 1831, when he applied for land in Austin's colony. Patrick Jack and his brother William, natives of Georgia, were considered able lawyers by their contemporaries; both served as judges during the early years of the Republic of Texas. In later years supporters of Travis and Jack said that during this period they were in the Atascosito neighborhood, where they were learning Spanish and endeavoring

[69] J. D. Bradburn to Inhabitants, November 17, 1831, Spanish Archives, General Land Office, 53-184.

to master Mexican law, undertakings with which neither Bradburn nor Mier y Terán would have quarreled.[70] The two would soon bring about Bradburn's downfall.

Reluctantly, because he knew that it would antagonize the Anglo-American community, Mier y Terán finally admitted that the only way for the central government to control and then eliminate the increasing federalism in Liberty was to eradicate the town and invest Anahuac as the seat of government for the Atascosito District. By divesting Liberty of its court and placing the *ayuntamiento* at Anahuac, the military commander could more easily supervise the contentious lawyers, many of whom were members of the town council. While Mier y Terán and Bradburn must have discussed this alternative during the commandant's visit, Mier y Terán did not draft the *oficio* until December 9, when he was homeward bound. Although no formal order was issued until December 9, the impending removal of the *ayuntamiento* was common knowledge by November 28, when Father Michael Muldoon, the curate of Austin's colony who had been visiting his friend Mier y Terán, wrote to Austin that "the municipality of Liberty was broken up. Anahuac is, of course, the capital." This was four days after Mier y Terán's departure and eleven days before the general's directive to Bradburn to order the elec-

[70]Muldoon to S. F. Austin, November 18, 1831, *Austin Papers* 2:711–12; J. D. Bradburn to alcalde, December 9, 10, 1831, Spanish Archives, General Land Office, 53:178–83; Archie P. McDonald, *Travis*, pp. 46–47, 54. Both Jacks received land in Austin's colony in March and April, 1831; W. H. Jack practiced law in San Felipe and Brazoria, and P. C. Jack became district judge of Harris and Galveston counties in 1840.

tion of officers for the *ayuntamiento* at Anahuac because Liberty, being in the littoral reserve, lacked permission from the supreme government for its existence.[71]

The November order for the residents to submit to Bradburn documents concerning their land had caused a flurry of activity and probably a great deal of grumbling. The orders of December 9 and 10, asking for the lawyers' credentials and moving the seat of government from Liberty to Anahuac, aroused their anger. After receiving Mier y Terán's order, Hugh B. Johnston, the alcalde at Liberty, immediately wrote to the *jefe* asking for instructions. In early January, with the aid of Father Muldoon and others who wanted the matter settled amicably, elections were held in both towns for a new *ayuntamiento* in Anahuac. Bradburn scarcely approved when John A. Williams was elected alcalde, Dr. George M. Patrick and John Lindsay *regidores* (councilmen), and John York prosecuting attorney. There was little that the colonel could do about the election of his enemies except for Williams, against whom a legal suit was pending for his activities of the previous year.[72] Bradburn finally acquiesced in the matter of the civil officers to maintain harmony.

General Mier y Terán had left Anahuac on the brig *Constante*, but the large copper-bottomed ship

[71] Commandant General to [Bradburn], December 9, 1831, Spanish Archives, General Land Office, 53:178–83; Muldoon to S. F. Austin, November 28, 1831, *Austin Papers*, 2:711–12.

[72] Hugh B. Johnston to Ramón Músquiz, December 18, 1831, Spanish Archives, General Land Office, 53:178–83; Johnston to Músquiz, December 11, 1831, Béxar Archives roll 146, frame 0190; J. D. Bradburn to Mier y Terán, January 8, 1832, Wagner Collection. The name of the town's lawyer looks like "A. J. Gurt," but "York" is more logical.

stuck fast on Red Fish Reef during a storm and eventually had to be abandoned. The general sent word to Anahuac about his predicament, and Fisher soon arrived aboard the port schooner to rescue him. While the transfer from brig to schooner was in progress, an inbound trading vessel, the *Exert*, came up the bay. The fifty-three-ton schooner had left New York on November 4 with owner James Reid, of New Orleans, on board and a cargo of goods destined for the store he had established a few months before in Anahuac in partnership with James Morgan, also of New Orleans. Fisher stopped the vessel for inspection, partly to impress Mier y Terán with the difficulties that he encountered with foreign captains. He demanded tonnage and tariff on some of the goods, but Reid protested, saying that having been en route to and from New York, he had been unaware of the establishment of the customhouse. Like others, he probably insisted that the law enforcement was ex post facto because he did not know about it before loading for Texas. Fisher estimated the duties based on a $5,000 evaluation, but with the general's intercession the pair finally agreed that Reid would pay one-fifth that amount upon arrival in Anahuac.[73]

Both vessels sailed on to Anahuac, where Mier y Terán remained until at least December 9, when he chartered the United States schooner *Topaz* to take him to Matamoros. When the *Exert* arrived, apparently after Mier y Terán's departure, Fisher impounded the vessel until Reid paid the duties in full

[73] Notes on Anahuac, *Lamar Papers*, 5:352; Notes from James Morgan, 1853, ibid., 4, pt. 1, pp. 298–300.

based on the $5,000 valuation. Morgan, in 1853, re-called that he had objected to the appraisal and had demanded instead a board of arbitration, to which Fisher had agreed. Two appraisers, one selected by Fisher and the other by Morgan, evaluated the cargo, but the figure was too low to suit Fisher. Morgan then appeared at the customhouse with a gun and de-manded his goods; the collector retreated into his of-fice, barred the door, and called for assistance from Bradburn. When the colonel arrived, he tried to calm Morgan, who was threatening to arm his slaves to re-cover his goods, a threat supported by the townspeo-ple. Bradburn finally convinced Morgan that if he would be patient the ultimate decision would be in his favor, and a few days later, when Fisher was absent, the colonel named Lt. José María Jiménez of the ma-rines to evaluate the goods one more time. The ref-eree set a compromise figure of $2,000 on the mer-chandise, and, while that did not completely satisfy Morgan, it settled the matter temporarily. That Mor-gan, Bradburn, and Fisher were all Masons has been overlooked, and it may be that this brotherhood of the men figured in the resolution of the touchy problem.[74]

Bradburn's decision to allow the cargo to land without Fisher's approval led to a break in their rela-tionship. Fisher protested that the military had no command over his office, but Bradburn replied that he was supreme over all matters in the Galveston Bay

[74]Notes from James Morgan, 1853, *Lamar Papers*, 4, pt. 1, pp. 298–300; J. D. Bradburn to Mier y Terán, January 8, 1832, Wagner Collection; Carter, *Masonry in Texas*, p. 245; *Louisiana Advertiser*, March 23, 1832.

area. In this instance the colonel courted favorable public opinion at the expense of the customs collector, because the townspeople wanted and needed the goods from the *Exert*. The bad feeling between Bradburn and Fisher increased, and in January the colonel ordered Fisher to move immediately to his new headquarters, which were being prepared at the eastern end of Galveston Island. Fisher, however, felt unable to leave Anahuac until the expected additional troops arrived because he believed that his life was in danger from Morgan, other local men, and a number of residents on the Brazos.[75]

While the settlers in the Atascosito District bore the main burden of Mier y Terán's orders, those living along the Brazos became incensed over Fisher's November order requiring all ships to call at Anahuac. At least three schooners were at Brazoria, the head of navigation about thirty miles from the mouth, when the restrictive *oficio* arrived. Until then the handful of soldiers stationed at the palmeto-log barracks on the eastern margin of the river near the beach had done little more than politely inquire for passports and the tonnage of vessels.[76] The twenty additional troops sent by Bradburn gave the little station a somewhat more impressive air, but since it lacked fort or cannon, few members of the Anglo communty respected the authority that the garrison was supposed to represent.

[75] Notes from James Morgan, 1853, *Lamar Papers*, 4, pt. 1, pp. 298–300; Notes from G. B. McKinstry, ibid., 3:242–43; Notes on Anahuac, ibid., 5:352; Bradburn to Mier y Terán, January 8, 1832, Wagner Collection.
[76] Holley, *Texas*, pp. 23–24, 29.

A series of meetings took place in Brazoria as a result of Fisher's announcement, and several captains and merchants spoke heatedly about the retroactive law and capricious government policies. Even Stephen F. Austin, who usually tried to calm any opposition to the government, joined in the loud, emotional denunciations of Fisher's seemingly arbitrary order. The furor was directed as much against Fisher personally as against the central government, and most captains and cargo owners declared that they would ignore the order either by offering a fee to the officer in charge at the mouth of the river or by passing without stopping. Three of the vessels had called at Brazoria before; two were owned at least in part by Brazoria residents, and one captain lived there. About December 15, Edwin Waller and William H. Wharton, owners of the *Sabine*, offered to pay $50 duty to Lt. Ignacio Domínguez, Bradburn's former adjutant, who now commanded the small garrison. He refused the "bribe" but, as Waller recalled many years later, asked for a duty of $100, which Waller declined to pay. The two owners then ordered Capt. Jeremiah Brown to run the "blockade," which he did by asking the passengers to go below and hoisting all the sails. The troops fired at the passing vessel, but no damage was done because the decks were loaded with bales of cotton, which absorbed the bullets. Lt. Domínguez arrested Waller and Wharton, but was forced to release them owing to the rising public outcry against military arrests of civilians. The *Spica* and the *Nelson* followed Brown's example before the end of December; the *Spica* stopped, but Capt. Isaiah

Doane, of Boston, former commander of a United States revenue cutter, refused to pay and sailed out into the Gulf. A shot from the garrison nicked Capt. Samuel Fuller of the *Nelson* when he attempted to pass the garrison, and he called for his rifle. One of the passengers, Spencer H. Jack, the younger brother of William H. and Patrick C. Jack, seized it and fired, wounding one of the guards. This act drawing blood was the final straw for Mier y Terán, who became adamant about his plan to tighten control over the Texans. Three schooners from New Orleans entered the Brazos on December 27 and went upriver to Brazoria without incident because, after the exchange of shots and the wounding of the guard, John Austin, still acting captain of the port, had ordered Domínguez to allow passage pending further orders, a course recommended by his cousin the empresario.[77]

At a protest meeting held on December 16 at Brazoria, George B. McKinstry and Branch T. Archer, both Masons, were selected to carry a petition to Fisher

[77] S. F. Austin to Emily M. Perry, December 23, 1831; S. F. Austin to J. D. Bradburn, December 30, 1831; S. F. Austin to Mary A. Holley, January 4, 14, 1832; S. F. Austin to Mier y Terán, January 8, 1832; S. F. Austin to J. F. Perry, December 27, 1831, *Austin Papers*, 2:725, 726, 731–34, 736–38; John Austin to J. D. Bradburn, December 27, 1831, Wagner Collection; J. D. Bradburn to Francisco Pizarro Martínez, February 29, 1832; Francisco Pizarro Martínez to Secretario de relaciones, February 6, March 22, 1832, Archivo fomento, Relaciones exteriores, Asuntos Varios, 1825–1849, 2d ser., Caja, 1830–34, Eugene C. Barker transcript, 566; hereafter cited as Fomento, Asuntos Varios, Barker transcript. There are some odd discrepancies: in reports to officials the *Spica* is not mentioned as violating Mexican law, yet it sailed about the same time; official reports mention the *Nelson*, the *Sabine*, and the *William A. Tyson*, yet Austin never refers to the *Tyson*. It was owned in part by James Breedlove, formerly Mexican consul in New Orleans. Information about the ships is from WPA, *Ship Registers and Enrollments of New Orleans, Louisiana, 1821–1830*, and *1831–1840*, vols. 2, 3.

asking him to rescind his order. McKinstry had been in the coasting trade for a number of years and in June, 1830, had served George Fisher as deputy collector. Fisher, however, refused to receive the petition, saying that he was powerless in the matter because the order had come from Mier y Terán. Until Duclor arrived, therefore, the papers had to be cleared at Anahuac. The pair then turned to Bradburn for relief, and he received their petition, agreeing that Fisher's order created difficulties for those on the Brazos. He promised to relieve the situation and in a few days sent Lt. Pacho to the Brazos to administer the duties, a step that Fisher could easily have taken.[78]

Bradburn received two letters from the two Austins during the first week in January in which the port captain and the empresario explained their roles in the recent violence at the mouth of the river. John Austin asked Bradburn to intercede with Fisher to permit incoming vessels to pick up a guard at the Brazos sandbar and then proceed upriver to discharge their cargoes under the soldier's supervision. Stephen F. Austin deplored Fisher's "impractical" regulation, which could not be enforced. While Domínguez had carried out his orders, the tiny garrison and even Fisher, at Anahuac, were subject to attacks by irate Brazorians. "*You* know your native countrymen," said Austin, adding: "I cannot understand the policy that is pursued as to Texas, if you understand it, I wish you would explain it to me. This is no time for

[78] Foote, *Texas and the Texans*, 2:14, 15; Yoakum, *History of Texas*, 1:281; Note from G. B. McKinstry, *Lamar Papers*, 3:242; Bradburn to Mier y Terán, January 8, 1832, Wagner Collection.

ambiguity, for it will require all our management united to keep things quiet unless a more Liberal System is adopted towards the people." The empresario urged suspension of customs duties on the Brazos, a suggestion that he had already made to Domínguez. Bradburn immediately forwarded to Mier y Terán a copy of Austin's critical letter with its conspiratorial tone of "us Anglos" against "those unreasonable Mexican orders," knowing that the commandant general would be angry. Austin failed to write the general until January 8 and then omitted saying anything about his advice to Domínguez. Mier y Terán reacted promptly. He sent Austin a sharp reprimand reminding the empresario that tariff was collected by every nation in the world but that only in Brazoria did it cause rioting.[79]

Until then the correspondence between the empresario and Bradburn had been cordial, but this incident appears to have been the turning point in their relationship. Bradburn, instead of being the gentleman that Austin had described to S. Rhoads Fisher one year before, had now become, in Austin's view, a tyrant, arrogant and despotic. Within six months Austin was calling Bradburn "incompetent" and "half crazy."[80]

Impelled by the recent events, Bradburn has-

[79] John Austin to J. D. Bradburn, December 27, 1831, Wagner Collection; S. F. Austin to J. D. Bradburn, December 30, 1831, *Austin Papers*, 2:781–82; J. D. Bradburn to Mier y Terán, January 8, 1832, Wagner Collection; S. F. Austin to Mier y Terán, January 8, 1832; Mier y Terán to S. F. Austin, January 27, 1832, *Austin Papers*, 2:733–35, 742–44.

[80] S. Rhoads Fisher to S. F. Austin, January 10, 1831, *Austin Papers*, 2:583–84; S. F. Austin to S. M. Williams, June 20, 1832, Williams papers.

tened to complete his fort. An extreme cold spell early in January, 1832, delayed brickmaking in the new kiln, but he managed to recover the cannon from the abandoned *Constante* and mount it at Anahuac. Terán had ordered him to buy the two cannons warehoused at Brazoria, pieces left by Henry Austin in 1830 in an unsuccessful attempt to lighten his steamboat to cross the Brazos sandbar. Not only did the fort at Anahuac need firepower, but cannons in the hands of the Anglo community were dangerous. The plan failed because the custodian at Brazoria refused to relinquish the two cannons. By February the garrison at Anahuac housed 215 men, though a few were on duty on the Brazos. Bradburn and Fisher continued to be at odds, and the colonel told Mier y Terán that Fisher was angry because he had ordered Lt. Pacho to the Brazos.[81]

In an effort to resolve the difficulty with the customhouse, Bradburn, Fisher, and Austin planned a meeting in late January, but at the last minute Fisher declined to participate in the session, held at the house of William Scott on the San Jacinto. Austin and Bradburn agreed that Fisher was the cause of the commotion, and they believed that if he was removed the unrest would disappear. Probably neither man totally believed that the solution was that simple, but Fisher was a convenient scapegoat for their growing problems. That was the last time the pair met. Austin

[81] J. D. Bradburn to Mier y Terán, January 8, 1832, Wagner Collection. See also Governor Letona to Ramón Músquiz, February 25, 1832; Alcalde Horatio Chriesman to R. Músquiz, April 26, 1832, Nacogdoches Archives, Blake Collection, 12:303, 314–15.

hurried back to San Felipe to prepare for his journey to Saltillo for the spring session of the legislature. The empresario recalled later (after Bradburn had left Texas) that the colonel had promised him to respect civil authority and to conciliate the people at Anahuac. Such an agreement was scarcely in keeping with Bradburn's view of the duties of a military commander and was probably a unilateral assumption by Austin. Austin added in a letter of July, 1832, to Samuel May Williams that Bradburn had reneged on his promise because he was "the most consumate of all fools" and "too much of a jack ass to be governed by reason or judgment."[82]

Two separate occurrences in January, 1832, caused both Bradburn and Mier y Terán a great deal of uneasiness throughout the spring. Bradburn received a list naming ten men on the Brazos who wanted to separate Texas from Mexico. The colonel sent a copy to Mier y Terán and also prepared one to be given to Domingo de Ugartechea, the new second-in-command who was to arrive in March to take command of the Brazos district.[83] Bradburn became increasingly obsessed about the Anglo-Americans and their intentions, believing that every event was part of a conspiracy to detach Texas. Mier y Terán faced an even greater danger when Santa Anna denounced

[82] S. F. Austin to Mier y Terán, February 5, 1832, *Austin Papers*, 2:747; "Bradburn Memorial"; S. F. Austin to S. M. Williams, July 19, 1832, Williams Papers; S. F. Austin to Charles G. Sayre, February 6, 1832, *Southwestern Historical Quarterly* 63 (January, 1960):454–56.

[83] J. D. Bradburn to Mier y Terán, January 8, 1832, Wagner Collection; "Bradburn Memorial"; Domingo de Ugartechea to Antonio Elosúa, March 13, 1832, Béxar Archives, roll 148, frame 0602.

the dictatoral Bustamante regime on January 2 and called for a coalition of Federalists to join him in a return to the republican principles of the Constitution of 1824. His Plan de Vera Cruz demanded the ouster of Lucas Alamán and the other conservative ministers. Mier y Terán, fearing that the Anglo-Texans would be attracted to the movement, urged Bradburn to do everything he could to prevent such a union.

Ugartechea's presence at the mouth of the Brazos was expected to calm the residents because he was more experienced and diplomatic than either Lt. Domínguez or Lt. Pacho. By the third week in March, Ugartechea, accompanied by Francisco Duclor, the customs collector, had reached his destination on the eastern bank of the Brazos with 100 troops, one six-pound cannon, and all the materials needed to build the small fort, to be named Velasco. Fisher had already ordered repairs made to the old building that was being used as a customhouse and had also contracted for a new office, a ferryboat, and a warehouse. By May the little fort was complete, and the mounted cannon commanded not only vessels crossing the bar but also all the private buidings on the point of land near the entrance to the river.[84]

By April, Fisher had moved from Anahuac to Galveston Island, where contractors William P. Harris and Robert Wilson had completed a customhouse, a

[84]George Fisher to W. P. Harris, March 20, 1832, Ugartechea to Elosúa, March 13, 1832, Béxar Archives, Blake Collection, Supplement, 9:253; Ugartechea to Elosúa, May 15, 1832, Béxar Archives, roll 150, frame 0029; A. Mitchell to W. H. Wharton, June 20, 1832, *Lamar Papers*, 1:98–99.

barracks, a warehouse, and other necessary outbuildings on the northeastern end of the island. Bradburn was glad that Fisher had left Anahuac because he had been the focus of so much hostility. The San Felipe *ayuntamiento* had petitioned the governor asking that the state intercede with the central government to replace Fisher with a native-born collector. Rumors spread that Fisher had misappropriated customhouse receipts, but the unhappy collector successfully defended his accounts, explaining that Mier y Terán had told him to use the receipts to build the various buildings at Galveston and on the Brazos.[85]

Fisher, still fearing for his life, asked Mier y Terán to transfer him to the customhouse at Matamoros. Since the request had to be approved in Mexico City, permission did not arrive until May, and Fisher finally departed on June 6, leaving Lt. Juan Cortina, his assistant, in charge of the customhouse. Responsibility for collecting customs on the Brazos remained in the hands of Duclor.[86]

With Fisher gone, Bradburn's enemies could concentrate on the commandant. The eleven newly arrived convict soldiers provided a convenient issue in April, when two of them attacked an Anglo woman, and a neighbor apparently failed to come to her rescue. The men of the community seized the neighbor, tarred and feathered him, and tried to do the same to the two soldiers. Bradburn, of course, disapproved of

[85] George Fisher to W. P. Harris, March 20, 1832, Franklin Papers; Letts, "George Fisher," pp. 96–97.

[86] Letts, "George Fisher," pp. 101–103.

the mob's action and refused to surrender his troops for Anglo frontier justice. The members of the newly formed vigilance committee then organized themselves into a military company and elected Patrick C. Jack captain. They announced that their intent was to protect settlers from the Indians, but the claim was obviously an excuse to cover activities aimed against Bradburn. The only Indians in the vicinity were the peaceful Alabamas-Coushattas. If the community had needed protection, Bradburn's troops were more than adequate. If he had needed civilian volunteers, he had the power to organize a militia with the aid of the alcalde. A militia created by local residents was in violation of Mexican law and, in Bradburn's eyes, constituted an illegal force intent on rebellion. Bradburn arrested Jack and, fearing that Jack's friends might release him from the fort jail, placed him with an armed guard aboard a schooner lying in the harbor.[87]

Robert McAlpin Williamson, a lawyer from San Felipe and one of the Brazos River agitators, visited Bradburn three times that same day trying to get Jack released. During the last interview Williamson became extremely angry and shouted that if Jack was not released he would kill Bradburn. Either to save face or to avert an incident, Bradburn replied that Jack's release was scheduled for 3:00 P.M. Jack's

[87]Rowe, "Disturbances at Anahuac," p. 280; J. D. Bradburn to Mier y Terán, June 1, 1832, Nacogdoches Archives, Blake Collection, 12:319–20; Nicholas D. Labadie, "Narrative of the Anahuac, or Opening Campaign of the Texas Revolution," in *The Texas Almanac for 1859*, in Day, comp., *The Texas Almanac, 1847–1873*, p. 128; hereafter cited as Labadie, "Narrative." For legal cause see Appendix 2 of this book.

friends hurried down to the landing and formed two lines. When their hero appeared, Dr. George M. Patrick, *regidor* and second-in-command of the military group, welcomed him ceremoniously, presenting him with a rusty sword amid rousing cheers and waving of hats. Bradburn correctly assumed that the demonstration was contrived to embarrass him and dismissed Patrick from his position as surveyor for the municipality, an appointive position over which the colonel had control.[88]

At this time there was a great deal of talk in Texas and even in the United States about Bradburn's role in punishing the American mutineers aboard the United States schooner *Topaz*. Mier y Terán had chartered the vessel at Harrisburg in December to return him to Matamoros after the grounding of the *Constante* and had arranged for Captain Rider to take Domingo de Ugartechea and about 100 troops from the Rio Grande to Anahuac on the return voyage. In February, 1832, off Galveston Island, the American crew took advantage of rough seas to mutiny, throwing Rider and the steersman overboard in a plot to confiscate about $3,000 that the captain had in his possession. The small crew of eight to ten men tricked the Mexican troops into going below decks by telling them that a terrible storm was coming. Once the deck was cleared, the mutineers sealed the hatches. After forcing the deck officers overboard, the mate led the crew toward the captain's cabin, where they intended to kill Ugartechea and the three other Mexican of-

[88] Labadie, "Narrative," pp. 128–29.

ficers before stealing the money and shoving off in the captain's gig—first scuttling the vessel to destroy the evidence of their misdeeds. The Mexican soldiers, realizing that treachery was afoot, broke out of the hold and quickly overpowered the crew except for the mate, who climbed into the rigging. Ugartechea ordered someone, probably an officer, to shoot him down, and Lt. of Marines José María Jiménez, who knew how to sail a vessel, assumed command and successfully guided the *Topaz* to Anahuac, where Bradburn put the crew in jail. Capt. Rider's money was also turned over to Bradburn, who made official reports to Mier y Terán. What became of the specie is unclear, and in his memorial Bradburn failed to mention it, merely referring to the reports he made to the commandant general.[89]

Bradburn and Jiménez quarreled about the disposition of the *Topaz*. The lieutenant wanted to deliver it to Harrisburg, to Rider's warehouse, but Bradburn needed it to take Ugartechea and the troops to the Brazos, and because of his rank, Bradburn prevailed. In March, 1832, after landing Ugartechea, the troops, and the supplies to build Fort Velasco, the *Topaz* foundered on the Brazos bar and apparently broke up.[90]

In the meantime the mutineers in jail at Anahuac attracted the attention of sympathetic residents, who visited them with food and tobacco. Playing on their common nationality, the sailors denied that they had

<hr/>

[89] John Irwin to Editor of *New York Daily Advertiser*, June 2, 1832, in *Louisiana Advertiser*, June 22, 1832; "Bradburn Memorial."
[90] "Bradburn Memorial"; *Lamar Papers*, 5:352.

mutinied and placed responsibility for the death of Capt. Rider and the mate on the Mexican soldiers. Always eager to blame Bradburn and the military, the residents of Anahuac accepted the tale and began writing friends in the United States about the outrage and how Bradburn "found it convenient" to believe the story about the crew's mutiny to justify confiscating the vessel and the money for his own use. A letter from "An American Citizen" appeared in the *New Orleans Louisiana Advertiser* of May 10, 1832, claiming that the charges against the American sailors were "false" and "impossible." The letter charged that Bradburn had confined the unfortunate men in a small room with sixty to eighty convicts and had even denied them the food and medicine offered by residents of Anahuac—and one was dying of scurvy. The writer urged authorities in the United States to investigate the matter because the sailors could not receive a fair trial from Bradburn, and if official appeals failed, citizens of Louisiana should cross the Sabine and rescue the unfortunates. A footnote added that Bradburn had detained runaway Louisiana slaves for his own work projects, a sensitive subject among local slaveholders. The letter reads very much as though it had been written by William Barret Travis or one of his friends.[91]

Five weeks later the *Louisiana Advertiser* published a rebuttal from a "reputable New Yorker," John

[91] *Louisiana Advertiser*, May 10, 1832. This letter, by "An American Citizen," could have been written in either New Orleans or Texas, but the information probably arrived on the schooner *Elizabeth* direct from the Brazos on May 10. See the text paragraph below about the letter from Ballou.

Irwin, who had been in Matamoros when the official reports about the *Topaz* had arrived and had personally perused the documents. Irwin denied stories in New York papers giving credence to the testimony of the American crew members and criticizing Bradburn. He detailed the events as reported by the Mexican officers and soldiers aboard the *Topaz* and added that Bradburn was held in "high repute" by the authorities in Matamoros.[92] Whether or not Irwin's letter, published on June 22 in New Orleans, had any effect on sentiment in the Crescent City cannot be determined, but his account was too late for the Texans, who by that date were massing on the Trinity.

Much of the antipathy toward Bradburn rested on his enforcement of the national law against slavery. While both the national and the state constitutions avoided banning slavery completely, Mexicans as a whole deplored the system of black slavery in the United States (while closing their eyes to their own system of debt peonage, which kept families bound to the land in perpetuity). To attract Anglo-American planters to develop Texas cotton lands, the officials had allowed Austin's colonists to bring their slaves with them as indentured servants, a nicety that salved Mexican consciences while permitting ninety-nine-year contracts providing low wages and high upkeep costs and, in effect, condoning perpetual slavery. Bradburn maintained that the exceptions granted to Austin's colony regarding slavery were not in effect outside his empresario grant; therefore, Liberty and

[92] John Irwin to Editor of *New York Daily Advertiser*, June 2, 1832, in *Louisiana Advertiser*, June 22, 1832.

Anahuac, being in the coastal reserve, were subject to the law as written, which declared that after 1829 slavery was not permitted anywhere in the republic. Austin, however, had managed to secure the exemption for his colony, and most Texans interpreted it to apply to all of Texas. Thus the residents were angry when two runaway slaves from Louisiana appeared in Anahuac in August, 1831, and Bradburn granted them asylum and put them to work, perhaps without wages, building the fort. For a while James Morgan had leased some of his slaves to Bradburn for that purpose, but after his confrontation with Fisher over duties on the *Exert* cargo, he withdrew the slaves.[93] Like other slaveholders, he worried that his blacks might learn that by law they were free in Mexico and could seek asylum in the fort.

When Mier y Terán visited Anahuac in November, William M. Logan arrived from Louisiana to claim the runaways. Mier y Terán ruled that Logan's only recourse was through diplomatic channels in Washington, D.C., and Mexico City, explaining that frontier military commanders lacked authority to release former slaves. The matter dragged on, and Logan employed William Barret Travis to handle the case. Bradburn proved adamant, however, insisting that the two blacks had joined the army and had applied for citizenship. Unable to resolve the problem through legal means, Travis and his colleague Warren D. C. Hall (who had known Bradburn in Louisiana) decided on subterfuge. Late one night during the

<hr/>

[93] Labadie, "Narrative," pp. 129–30; Monroe Edwards to R. M. Williamson, May 24, 1832, *Lamar Papers*, 1:91–92; "Bradburn Memorial."

second week in May, 1832, a tall man swathed in a cloak approached the sentry with a letter for Bradburn, which was delivered the following morning. The note was signed "Ballou," the name of a former member of Jean Laffite's pirate crew who had settled on the old smuggling trail northeast of Anahuac. The letter warned Bradburn that 100 armed men were poised in Louisiana ready to cross the Sabine to rescue the two slaves. Already obsessed about possible attacks by filibustering parties favoring independence for Texas, Bradburn accepted the letter without question and dispatched scouting parties. A day or two later, when all of them returned and reported that they had found no armed men between the Trinity and Sabine rivers and that no one had even heard rumors of such an invasion, the commandant realized that he had been duped. Suspecting Travis of engineering the hoax, on May 17 or 18 he sent a patrol to arrest Travis at his law office and conduct him to the fort for questioning.[94]

The American community reacted in a predictable manner. Accustomed to the protections guaranteed by the first ten amendments to the United States Constitution—a warrant for an arrest, a statement of charges against the accused, bail, and a trial by jury— they refused to believe that the Republic of Mexico did not provide the same safeguards. How could a military force arrest a civilian without a warrant? How could they hold him incommunicado without charging him or setting bail? Bradburn's actions appeared

[94]*Ibid.*

arbitrary and despotic to those who refused to understand Mexican law.

Patrick Jack, who as a practicing attorney in Anahuac should have know Mexican law, stormed into Bradburn's office and demanded Travis's release, undoubtedly using abusive language and making threats to call up his irregular militiamen. Bradburn immediately arrested Jack too, and by May 18 both were in the barracks' *carcel*. Bradburn acted correctly, following both civil and military codes. As the military commander in the federal reserve along the coast, he had the power to arrest anyone involved in conspiracy against the government or its officers. If the culprits had been soldiers, the punishment would have been death by hanging, but because they were civilians Bradburn intended to send them to Matamoros, where the commandant general would decide their case.[95]

Bradburn tried to isolate the prisoners, but one of James Morgan's slaves, Harriet, carried messages in and out as she delivered their food and laundry. An alert sentry stopped Harriet on May 24 and confiscated a note arranging for an escape two nights later. To make the pair's imprisonment more secure, Bradburn transferred them to the recently emptied new brick kiln, which he had ordered altered for their use, placed two cannons facing the access to their "dungeon," and increased the guard. Learning that Monroe Edwards, a clerk at Morgan and Reid's store, had planned their deliverance and passed notes in to

[95] Ministerio de Guerra y Marina, *Ordenanza militar para el régimen, disciplina, subordinación y servicio del ejército*, 2:230.

the prisoners, the colonel ordered him arrested and placed in the brick kiln also.[96]

When he heard that his brother had been arrested, William H. Jack left Brazoria in a yawl. If he sailed through the shallow bays between the mainland and San Luís and Galveston islands, he probably reached Anahuac within twenty-four hours. Lt. Pacho, Bradburn's assistant and the prosecutor of the case against Travis and Jack, at first refused to let Jack visit the prisoners. The usually mild-mannered Jack, who wore thick glasses and was not robust, became belligerent and Pacho finally permitted him a brief interview. When Jack returned to his yawl, he promised local supporters that he would return as soon as possible with armed men to secure the release of the prisoners.[97]

Bradburn was either absent or chose to delegate his authority during Jack's visit. On June 1 he wrote to Mier y Terán about the arrests but said nothing about Jack's demands. While Lt. Pacho believed that an armed force was en route from the Brazos and that the prisoners were plotting independence, Bradburn, uncharacteristically, told the commandant general that he doubted the rumor but added that perhaps he would need reinforcements in the near future.[98] One can only assume that the statement was designed to give Mier y Terán the impression that

[96] J. Lindsay to R. M. Williamson, May 18, 1832; Monroe Edwards to R. M. Williamson, May 24, 1832, *Lamar Papers*, 1:90–91; Labadie, "Narrative," pp. 130–31.
[97] Labadie, "Narrative," pp. 131–32.
[98] J. D. Bradburn to Mier y Terán, June 1, 1832, Nacogdoches Archives, Blake Collection, 12:319–20.

Bradburn was in control and not easily upset by mere rumor.

By June 4, a day or so after William H. Jack returned to the Brazos, small groups of angry citizens began marching toward Anahuac by way of Harrisburg and Liberty. Frank W. Johnson, former alcalde of San Felipe, led a group from that village, and messages were sent to other neighborhoods for volunteers to meet at Lynch's ferry. John Austin, in his office as second alcalde, gathered a force of about thirty from the Brazoria neighborhood, but before leaving the mouth of the river, he called on Ugartechea at Velasco to report the complaints and the contemplated action. Ugartechea listened sympathetically and agreed that Bradburn might have erred in judgment but said that, instead of promoting violence, Austin should ask the commandant at Anahuac to turn over the prisoners to the local civil authorities until Mier y Terán could rule on the matter. Ugartechea persuaded Austin to take with him Lt. Domínguez and about forty troops as a conciliatory gesture and to serve as Ugartechea's emissary. Upon reaching Anahuac, Austin and Domínguez called on Bradburn, but the colonel was not moved by the plea to turn the prisoners over to the civil authorities. He called his staff officers together and named Lt. Cortina to preside while Lt. Pacho presented the case against Travis and Jack. The adjutant explained that under Article 26 of the military laws governing the installation at Anahuac the accused had committed sedition and had fomented a rebellion against military authority. Under military law the prisoners had to be tried in a military court unless Mier y Terán ruled otherwise, and without such an order the officers at Anahuac could not release them to civil authority. Convinced of the legality of the procedures, Austin apologized and returned to the Brazos confident that petitions to Mier y Terán would solve the dilemma.[99]

About the time Austin left Anahuac, the officers discovered that someone had stolen several of their horses, an act that brought arrests of more men, including Samuel T. Allen and at least one other Anglo. The news about the additional incarcerations reached the Brazos the day after Austin returned, and the apparently arrogant action changed his mind. He hurried to join the volunteers on the Trinity. Johnson and the first contingent had reached Liberty, where they acquired additional recruits, and the little army camped at David Minchey's farm, a few miles below the village, to make their plans.[100]

Bradburn's chronic fear that the Texans were planning an uprising was about to be realized right under his nose. When he learned that the insurgents were camped on the Trinity, he sent his only cavalry company to reconnoiter. The entire troop of nine-

[99] R. M. Williamson, "Appeal," June 4, 1832; W. D. C. Hall to John Austin, June 4, 1832; J. S. Brown to W. H. Wharton, June 20, 1832, *Lamar Papers*, 1:92–93, 99; "Bradburn Memorial"; Ugartechea to A. Elosúa, June 7, 1832, in Elosúa to Músquiz, June 23, 1832, Nacogdoches Archives, Blake Collection, 12:332–33.

[100] "Bradburn Memorial"; J. S. Brown to W. H. Wharton, June 20, 1832, *Lamar Papers*, 1:99; Labadie, "Narrative," p. 132; Johnson, "Further Account . . . of the First Breaking Out of Hostilities," in *Texas Almanac for 1859*, in Day, comp., *Texas Almanac, 1857–1873*, p. 138; hereafter cited as Johnson, "Further Account."

teen rode into an ambush and surrendered without a shot being fired. The volunteers with their prisoners moved to White's crossing, on Turtle Bayou, about six miles north of Anahuac, where they made camp. They decided that it was time to organize their army and quickly elected Frank W. Johnson and Warren D. C. Hall their commanders.[101]

On the next day, June 10, the insurgents entered Anahuac and occupied the buildings on the north side previously used as troop barracks. About midday a committee composed of Johnson, John Austin, George B. McKinstry, H. K. Lewis, and Hugh B. Johnston, the former alcalde of Liberty, asked for an interview with Bradburn to repeat the demand for release of the prisoners to civil authority. They added that perhaps an arrangement could be made to exchange the prisoners for the cavalrymen. Bradburn again called for a staff meeting, and Pacho repeated his decision that the prisoners must stand military trial unless Mier y Terán intervened.[102]

Bradburn's decision to defer to his staff on both these occasions suggests that he wanted to avoid responsibility for causing a confrontation with the Anglo community and did not want to create a problem for himself among his officers. He had encountered difficulties with almost every officer over the building

[101] Rowe, "The Disturbances at Anahuac," p. 283; Scates, "Early History of Anahuac," p. 683; Johnson, "Further Account," p. 138; J. D. Bradburn to Francisco Pizarro Martínez, June 27, 1832, Fomento, Asuntos Varios, Barker transcript, 566:101. The dates cited for various events by the participants differ slightly; and they do not always agree with Vicente Filisola, *Memorias*, used by Rowe in her article.

[102] Rowe, "The Disturbances at Anahuac," p. 284; Johnson, "Further Account," p. 139.

of the fort. Evidently he was not a popular commander for reasons that are unclear—perhaps because he was a foreigner or because he was difficult to deal with. Some evidence exists that Bradburn had fallen under the influence of his secretary, García Ugarte, one of the convict soldiers, whom Piedras later described as a "criminal, wicked, intriguing, and seditious man."[103] Such an association may have turned the staff against its commander.

Morale at Anahuac declined in June, 1832, which Bradburn later explained in his memorial detailing his activities. He believed that the trouble stemmed from the neglect of the central government, which failed to send supplies and the payroll. The immediate cause of disaffection in June was the return of the schooner *Martha* from Matamoros without the ammunition and reinforcements for which Bradburn had sent it. Moreover, Mier y Terán had sent a gloomy message explaining his inability to provide the necessary aid because the Centralist forces under his command had suffered a serious defeat at Tampico and had lost control of the customhouse, the source of revenue for the payroll. Indeed, Mier y Terán became so despondent over these and other difficulties that he committed suicide on July 3.

The *Martha* arrived about the same time that the rebels appeared on the Trinity. On board were Lt. Col. Félix María Subarán and his sergeant, who had pronounced in favor of Santa Anna and the Plan de Vera Cruz and whom Mier y Terán had banished to

[103] Piedras to Elosua, July 12, 1832, Nacogdoches Archives, Blake Collection, 13:37–49.

the frontier as political prisoners. The commandant general little suspected when he ordered the pair to Fort Terán, near Nacogdoches, that the *santanistas* would subvert the restless garrison on Galveston Bay. Bradburn, faced with angry colonists and a demoralized staff, asked Subarán to accept the post of second-in-command, correctly assuming that the *santanista* would defend Texas against any effort to separate it from Mexico. Subarán agreed and attended the meeting with the insurgents on June 10, though he took no active part.[104]

Frank W. Johnson and the others left the unsatisfactory meeting with a threat to try violent action to recover their friends, and they spent the next day reconnoitering and skirmishing. John A. Williams, who had returned to Anahuac with Subarán on the *Martha*, approached his fellow countrymen with an offer from Bradburn and Subarán for a second conference. Williams explained that Subarán planned to win over the garrison to Santa Anna and that if he succeeded he would become the commander of Anahuac. In such a case Subarán would view the activities of the Texans as an attack against centralism. Moreover, Williams added, Subarán and the staff officers had told him to offer Travis, Jack, and the others in exchange for the cavalrymen and the rebels' promise

[104] "Bradburn Memorial"; Bradburn to Piedras, and in Piedras to Elosúa, June 23, 1832, Nacogdoches Archives, Blake Collection, 12:346. A translation of Bradburn's memorial names Sgt. Ocampo as the man accompanying Subarán. Carlos Ocampo, previously commanding the Fifth Company of the Twelfth Battalion at Nacogdoches, was in Anahuac by April, 1832, and commanded a company of the Twelfth there. He was still the commander in May, and thus it seeems impossible that he was in Matamoros at the end of the month awaiting banishment to the frontier.

to withdraw from Anahuac to Turtle Bayou. The Anglo prisoners would not be released, however, until both conditions were met.[105]

Some of the rebels doubted Williams's veracity and the trustworthiness of Bradburn and Subarán, but Wyly Martin, a veteran officer of the War of 1812, convinced them that an officer's word was sacred. Martin, Austin, and Liberty alcalde Johnston met with Subarán and the lieutenants and agreed to the terms. The Texans retreated to Turtle Bayou and released the cavalrymen. Anglo residents of Anahuac noted that after the rebels had retired from the former barracks on the north side of the village the troops emerged from the garrison, entered the barracks, and carried out clothing and ammunition that had been stored in the attic and had not been discovered by the rebels. Not all the Anglos withdrew from town. Frank W. Johnson remembered in 1859 that about fifteen to thirty remained in addition to the commissioners. Bradburn decided that their presence violated the terms of the agreement. The next morning he sent John Austin a message that the Anglos had broken the treaty and that therefore he would not release the prisoners. Moreover, he said, within two hours he intended to commence firing on the village. The insurgents, ignoring the fact that they had not strictly observed the terms agreed upon, later declared that Bradburn had concocted the cease-fire to get them out of town so that he could recover the stored ammunition. In subsequent retellings of the

[105] Johnson, "Further Account," p. 139.

incident, Bradburn's firing on the town was evidence of his innate treachery and despotism. By 1841, Foote was calling the colonel a "faithless miscreant" and referring to his "odious breach of faith," hyperbole that scarcely fits the facts.[106]

After learning of Bradburn's warning that the cannon would be trained on the buildings, women and children quickly bundled their possessions and headed up the road to Taylor White's ranch beyond Turtle Bayou. During the brief skirmish in Anahuac between the troops and the rebels, one Texan and five soldiers were killed. The insurgents then withdrew to Turtle Bayou, where they gathered in consultation and appointed a committee to draft a statement showing cause for their actions and also to accept the Plan of Vera Cruz. Adopted June 13, 1832, the Turtle Bayou Resolutions deplored the manner in which "the present dynasty" had violated the Constitution of 1824 by substituting military order for civil authority. As *freemen* devoted to the "correct interpretations and enforcement of the constitution and laws," they pledged their "lives and fortunes" to aid their "gallant" chieftain, Gen. Santa Anna, who was fighting to defend civil liberty. Finally, they called on the rest of Texas to join them. They sent John Austin and a force to the Brazos with a copy of the resolutions to enlist aid and to bring back four cannons stored at San Felipe and Brazoria with which to lay siege to Anahuac.[107]

[106] Ibid.; Labadie, "Narrative," pp. 132–33; Foote, *Texas and the Texans*, 2:17.
[107] Johnson, "Further Account," p. 140; Labadie, "Narrative," pp.

While waiting for the return of Austin with the cannons, the local men returned home to attend to their usual business, and those from the Brazos camped at Joseph Dunman's farm on the Trinity, about midway between Anahuac and Liberty. Bradburn's spies kept him informed about the rebels' activities, and he took advantage of the lull to strengthen his fort and to send messages to Colonel Piedras at Nacogdoches, a little over 200 miles to the north, and to Colonel Elosúa at San Antonio, about 300 miles to the west. Bradburn had only about 160 men at Anahuac and Ugartechea had about 60 at Velasco.[108]

Upon receiving the plea for help, Piedras forwarded a message to Colonel Francisco Ruíz at Tenoxtitlán to send part of his command to aid Bradburn. Ruíz was unable to comply owing to a shortage of horses and supplies. Piedras ordered two companies of his Twelfth Battalion and some cavalry troops to start south. He also called up the civil militia, securing only nineteen who could march, and set off toward Anahuac on June 19. At Fort Terán, about eighty miles below Nacogdoches, Piedras added previously detached cavalrymen to the outfit and with perhaps one hundred men, including nine Coushattas—about one-half of his entire force—moved southward. At Fort Terán, Piedras learned that the insurgents not only had demanded the return of the prisoners but had declared for the Plan of Vera Cruz,

133–34; Rowe, "The Disturbances at Anahuac," pp. 286–88; Holley, *Texas*, pp. 150–51; Scates, "Early History of Anahuac," p. 683.

[108]"Bradburn Memorial"; Rowe, "The Disturbances at Anahuac, p. 286; Johnson, "Further Account," p. 140.

thus precipitating him, a loyal Centralist officer, into the civil war. He was reluctant to leave the Nacogdoches neighborhood because rumors indicated that the Anglo-Americans living on Ayish Bayou, about thirty miles east of Nacogdoches, planned to join the insurgents on the Trinity. Ever since he assumed command at Nacogdoches in 1827, he had experienced a great deal of trouble with the Anglos in his district, and he did not relish the idea of an armed confrontation.[109]

While Piedras marched south, John Austin and his associates reached Brazoria, where the residents met on June 20 and declared themselves in opposition to the Bustamante regime and in favor of the Constitution of 1824, which they and the *santanistas* claimed had been destroyed by the administration. The next day Austin commandeered the schooner *Brazoria*, lined it with bales of cotton, and placed three cannons on board; the cannon from San Felipe was already en route with volunteers marching toward Anahuac. Expecting that Colonel Ugartechea would challenge their passage past the fort at Velasco, about 100 to 150 men accompanied the vessel downstream, 40 aboard the schooner and the rest marching by road. Although badly outnumbered, having only 64 infantry troops and 9 artillerymen, Ugartechea refused to join the rebellion when he was visited by a committee carrying a white flag. Austin finally attacked the small log fort on the night of June 26. The following morning, almost out of ammuni-

[109] Rowe, "The Disturbances at Anahuac," pp. 292–93; F. Ruíz to A. Elosúa, June 23, 1832, Nacogdoches Archives, Blake Collection, 12:345.

tion and with a number of men needing medical attention, Ugartechea capitulated to the insurgents with the understanding that he and his men would be immediately returned to Matamoros with their sidearms but would leave behind the cannon, the swivel gun, and any surplus arms. Cannon fire had damaged the *Brazoria*, however, and she was unable to take the Centralist troops to the Rio Grande.[110] By the time Austin had resolved the problems at the mouth of the Brazos, he learned that Bradburn had relinquished command at Anahuac and that the prisoners had been released, news that made his proposed voyage with the cannons unnecessary.

About the time that Austin was attacking Velasco, Piedras reached Aaron Cherry's house, about thirty miles north of Liberty. In anticipation of his arrival the rebels had posted a picket near the Menard Creek crossing, and when the troops appeared, the picket fell back to warn Johnson. Piedras, uneasy and believing that he was greatly outnumbered by the Anglo-Americans, sent a delegation to Johnson asking for the settlers' demands. His commissioners returned with a list of grievances against Bradburn and a request for an interview with Piedras. The Nacogdoches commandant still suspected treachery and refused a face-to-face meeting, but under such duress he acquiesced to most of the Texans' demands and sent the committee back with an agreement to be signed. Un-

[110] Citizen's Meeting, [ca. June 20, 1832]; John Austin to J. Rowland, June 21, 1832; John Austin to F. Duclor, June 21, 1832; Brazoria Militia, June 22–27, 1832; Report of Ugartechea, July 1, 1832, *Lamar Papers*, 1:97–101, 116, 132–36; Ugartechea to Elosúa, June 7, 1832 in Elosúa to Músquiz, June 18, 1832, Nacogdoches Archives, Blake Collection, 12:332.

der its terms he agreed to the following: the *ayuntamiento* at Liberty would be reestablished immediately, the civilian prisoners at Anahuac would be released to the civil authorities at Liberty, Bradburn would surrender his command to an officer of his choice, and, finally, the settlers could petition Mier y Terán to rectify injustices committed by Bradburn. These extremely favorable terms, granted even before he had had an opportunity to talk with Bradburn, indicated Piedras's eagerness to appease the rebels and avoid a confrontation that he feared he might lose. The insurgents quickly accepted the terms on June 28, and the commandant ratified them the following day. Piedras broke camp and marched to Anahuac, arriving on July 1.[111]

When Piedras arrived, Bradburn agreed to step down as commander at Anahuac to satisfy the *santanista* rebels in Texas. After consulting with his staff officers, Bradburn asked Subarán to assume command. Subarán, however, convinced that the fort was doomed and unsure of the support he might receive, declined in favor of Piedras.[112]

Thus it was Piedras, nominally in command, who released Travis, Jack, and the others on July 2 and turned them over to Alcalde Hugh B. Johnston, who had accompanied the colonel from Liberty. The Anglo party and the former prisoners, technically still under arrest, returned to Liberty. Within a week all

[111] Rowe, "The Disturbances at Anahuac," pp. 292–94; Bradburn to Francisco Pizarro Martínez, August 10, 1832, Fomenta, Asuntos Varios, Barker transcript, 566:104–105.
[112] "Bradburn Memorial."

were freed. Confident that they were superior to the Centralist forces and contemptuous of the Mexican officers, Travis and the others now devoted themselves to destroying Bradburn.[113]

Piedras remained at Anahuac until July 8, when he started back to Nacogdoches, where he rightly feared that a similar revolt might occur. Before leaving, he placed Lt. Cortina, the senior officer except for Subarán and Bradburn, in charge of the fort with instructions that in case of attack Bradburn was to resume command. Subarán was to remain for a few days, and then, on his honor, he was to follow Piedras to Nacogdoches. Piedras warned Bradburn and the others to act prudently to prolong the armistice that he had arranged in the hope that the settlers would remain calm. The senior officers, including Piedras, expected that the Centralist regime would soon recover from its recent setback and that the opportunity would come to make the Anglo-Texans "obey the laws and reduce them to the blindest obedience."[114] With that vindictive thought Piedras marched off to Nacogdoches, where on August 2 the local residents declared for Santa Anna and forced Piedras to withdraw with those troops who did not choose to defect.

On July 11, three days after Piedras's departure, the troops at Anahuac staged a drunken demonstration in the plaza and declared for Santa Anna. Unable to

[113] Rowe, "The Disturbances at Anahuac," p. 295.

[114] Piedras to Bradburn, July 4, 1832, Nacogdoches Archives, Blake Collection, 13:11–15; Rowe, "The Disturbances at Anahuac," pp. 295–96; "Bradburn Memorial."

control the mob, Cortina called on Bradburn to take command, but the colonel refused, knowing that his orders would have no effect. The soldiers shouted for Subarán, and Bradburn realistically advised Cortina to turn the command over to the *santanista* officer. Bradburn blamed Travis for the humiliating coup: he and other Anglos had come to the plaza and opened a barrel of whiskey, inviting the garrison to drink up and haranguing them to join Santa Anna's reform movement. Subarán, whose addiction to alcohol was well known, soon joined in the demonstration. Bradburn had feared such an occurrence, and he and Cortina had tried to find means to remove the troops from Anahuac, but they could find no boats to charter, and they knew that if they marched them overland the soldiers would desert.[115]

From the moment that he relinquished his command, Bradburn had believed that his life was in danger, and he had asked for a bodyguard. An abortive assassination attempt, attributed to Travis, convinced the colonel that he should leave Anahuac as soon as possible. Subarán, now in command, agreed and tried to hire a boat to take Bradburn to Matamoros or Vera Cruz, but the *santanista* ship captains, all Anglo-Texans, blockaded Anahuac and prevented Bradburn's escape by water. The colonel finally arranged for a guide to take him to Louisiana over the network of smuggling trails leading to the Sabine. On July 13, two days after the coup, Subarán warned the few re-

[115] J. Cortina to Piedras, July 15, 1832, Nacogdoches Archives, Blake Collection, Supplement, 17:233; J. Cortina to Félix María Subarán, July 15, 1832, Nacogdoches Archives, Blake Collection, 13:50.

maining Centralist officers that he could no longer guarantee their safety. After dark Bradburn and his guide left the fort, heading eastward, while the cavalry galloped off toward its home garrison at La Bahía. The other officers, Lts. Cortina, Montero, Landevaco, Domíngues, and Añorga, quit the fort and sought sanctuary with Alcalde Johnston at Liberty.[116] Some of the local residents, including, ironically, John A. Williams, refused to join the reform movement and gave assistance to the Centralist officers; these men were labeled "Tories" by their disbelieving neighbors.

Bradburn and his guide avoided the main road and took one of the parallel traces leading toward Opelousas, Louisiana. They probably crossed the Neches above present-day Beaumont, and the Sabine near the mouth of Quicksand Creek, in Newton County, where there was a ferry. Rumors circulated among Bradburn's enemies that he was pursued by eight men all the way to the Sabine, where they closed in, forcing him to abandon his horse and to swim the river to escape. In extant correspondence detailing his experiences to friends, the colonel failed to mention such an incident, saying only that the route between the Neches and the Sabine was dangerous. He added that he heard much talk of running the "Spaniards" out of Texas and that a justice of the peace in southwestern Louisiana boasted that he could raise four thousand men to invade Texas.[117]

---

[116] Rowe, "The Disturbances at Anahuac," p. 297; "Bradburn Memorial"; Labadie, "Narrative," p.136.

[117] Henry Morse to J. F. Perry, August 5, 1832, *Austin Papers*,

Bradburn arrived in New Orleans on August 6 and sought refuge with Francisco Pizarro Martínez, the Mexican consul, who lived on Chartres Street. The colonel prepared written accounts of his flight for transmittal to the authorities. He described the "rabble" that were proposing to invade Texas as fugitives from both civil justice and the United States Army. Bradburn believed that these men could be "un Ejército terrible."[118] Who should know better? Only sixteen years earlier Bradburn had been a member of a similar sort of army.

The colonel was not completely safe in the Crescent City, where early reports of the "revolution" in Texas had labeled him a tyrant. The rumors had reached New Orleans early in July and had been confirmed on July 13, when passengers from Brazoria brought copies of resolutions adopted there on June 24 and accounts of Ugartechea's capitulation three days later. The first reports said that the Texans had captured Bradburn and that he was in the hands of the civil authorities, awaiting trial for his despotic acts. A letter from Natchitoches reported that 120 men had attacked Bradburn for "inhumane treatment" of civilian prisoners "bordering on starvation," adding that Piedras and 100 troops and 118 Indians

---

2:831–32; J. D. Bradburn to Francisco Pizarro Martínez, August 10, 1832; Francisco Pizarro Martínez to Secretario de Relaciones, August 14, 1832, Fomento, Asuntos Varios, Barker transcript, 566:104–106.

[118]*Louisiana Advertiser*, July 13, 14, August 9, 1832; J. D. Bradburn to Francisco Pizarro Martínez, June 27, August 10, 1832; Francisco Pizarro Martínez to Secretario de Relaciones, August 14, 1832, Fomento, Asuntos Varios, Barker transcript, 566:101–106. Strangely, extant copies of the two New Orleans papers, the *Bee* and the *Courier*, do not mention Bradburn.

had marched immediately and that the whole country was under martial law. Sabine neighbors were "exasperated" and planned to attack the Mexicans. The most inflammatory account was contained in a letter dated July 8, apparently from Travis to a friend in New Orleans, in which he said that he and another lawyer had been jailed by Bradburn for their political opinions. The "tyrant" had agreed to exchange the writer for the cavalrymen but reneged at the last moment, when "300 flew to arms." The writer added that the "Mexicans have learned a lesson," that "Americans know their rights," and that constitutional and sacred guarantees are not "things to be broken and trampled under foot." Piedras, said the writer, had agreed to everything the Americans wanted, and John Austin, after reducing a "fort of great strength" at the mouth of the Brazos, was on his way to Anahuac with 250 men and four cannons. "The infamous Fisher and the still more infamous Bradburn have been removed from office" and their places taken by Don Juan Cortina, a man of the "highest integrity and honor."[119] The letter had been published on July 26, only ten days before Bradburn reached New Orleans, and had inflamed public opinion against the colonel.

On August 9 the *Advertiser* announced Bradburn's arrival in New Orleans and said that the colonel intended to go immediately to Mexico City to place before the government his documents concerning the recent events in Texas. The editor had seen

[119]*Louisiana Advertiser*, July 26, 1832.

Bradburn's papers, which, he said, certainly gave a different view of Texas affairs. Bradburn asked the American people to "suspend their opinions" until the Mexican authorities had had an opportunity to rule on the charges lodged against him. He probably had learned about Mier y Terán's suicide when he reached the Crescent City, though the news had been published there on July 20 and perhaps had circulated to settlements upriver, where he may have heard about the tragic event. It would, of course, affect his career.[120]

Bradburn prepared to leave for Matamoros on August 14, and the consul probably chartered a vessel to take him to the Rio Grande. Pizarro Martínez sent along his dispatches and included a copy of the July 23 issue of *Texas Gazette*, which described the honors accorded Col. José Antonio Mexía, the *santanista* officer who had sailed from Matamoros to the Brazos with a fleet of five vessels to quell any movement to- ward independence among the Texans. Mexía arrived on July 16, bringing with him Stephen F. Austin. John Austin and the others quickly explained that their activities at Velasco and Anahuac had been carried out in the name of Santa Anna, a ploy that Mexía accepted.[121]

Bradburn left New Orleans before news of Piedras's defeat at Nacogdoches on August 1 reached the city. The Centralist troops were forced to march to Béxar, and by the end of the month the civil govern-

[120] Ibid., July 20, August 9, 1832.
[121] F. Pizarro Martínez to Secretario de Relaciones, August 14, 1832, Fomento, Asuntos Varios, Barker transcript, 566:101–106.

ment in Texas had adopted the Plan of Vera Cruz, and all the troops who refused to join the movement marched south. Only Cortina, nominally collector of customs, and a few of his associates remained on Galveston Bay. Before he left Anahuac in July to join Mexía, Subarán tried to arrest Cortina and the other officers as deserters from Anahuac, but the Centralist officers were protected by Alcalde Johnston at his ranch. After all the troops had departed, Cortina moved to Galveston Island, ostensibly to keep the customhouse in operation. In September he allowed Duclor and Domínguez to abandon the Brazos and return to Tampico, though he and the others remained on the island until early 1833. Subarán's troops had severely damaged the fort at Anahuac in July, and in November someone set fire to remaining wooden structures. The ruins became materials for scavengers.[122]

When Bradburn returned to Matamoros, he perhaps learned that, on June 29, Mier y Terán, in his last order from his encampment at Croix before going to Padilla and his death, had appointed Ugartechea to replace Bradburn at Anahuac. Mier y Terán had received word of the trouble in Texas on June 25. Bowing to pressure from Stephen F. Austin (who had visited him during his withdrawal north from Tampico), Mier y Terán had abandoned Bradburn to ap-

[122] *Courier*, July 21, 1832; *Louisiana Advertiser*, August 23, 28, 1832; *Bee*, August 25, 1832; Rowe, "The Disturbances at Anahuac," pp. 297–98; Juan Cortina to F. M. Subarán, July 15, 1832, Nacogdoches Archives, Blake Collection, 13:50–52; Henry Morse to J. F. Perry, August 5, 1832; F. Duclor to Ayuntamiento of San Felipe, September 27, 1832, *Austin Papers*, 2:831, 867–68.

pease Anglo-Texan sentiment. The orders were sent on the *Exert*, which went aground a few days later but finally reached Galveston Bay after Ugartechea had surrendered and Bradburn had fled. No doubt word about the replacement leaked from Mier y Terán's headquarters after his suicide and spread among the other officers, including Mariano Paredes y Arillaga, Bradburn's brother-in-law, who had joined Mier y Terán's command in May and had led three hundred Centralist troops to Matamoros at the end of June to recapture the port for the administration.[123]

Bradburn's unhappy experience in Texas did not immediately injure his military career, because the struggle between the Centralists and the *santanista* Federalists continued, and his services were needed. By August Acting President Bustamante assumed personal command of the four thousand men who comprised the northern Centralist army, and under his leadership they occupied San Miguel de Grande (now Allende) and Dolores. Bradburn reached the Rio Grande in time to participate in a decisive battle on September 18, in which Bustamante defeated the much larger *santanista* force. Bradburn's service was outstanding, and on December 11, Bustamante breveted him brigadier general and gave him command of a regiment near Reynosa.[124]

[123] Mier y Terán to S. F. Austin and others, June 29, 1832, *Austin Papers*, 2:799; S. F. Austin to S. M. Williams, July 1, 2, 1832, Williams Papers; Juan Cortina to F. M. Subarán, July 15, 1832, Nacogdoches Archives, Blake Collection, 13:50–52: Morton, "Life of Mier y Terán," *Southwestern Historical Quarterly* 48 (July–October, 1944):537.

[124] Bancroft, *History of Mexico*, p. 421; Mestre Ghigliazza, comp., *Efemérides biográficas*, p. 33.

Early in December, 1832, Bustamante and Santa Anna entered negotiations to end the strife to "preserve the Constitution of 1824," and at the end of the month they signed an armistice that not only ended the fighting but also placed Manuel Gómez Pedraza in the executive seat to finish out the term to which he had been elected in 1828. Bradburn, following his commander's example and acting under his orders, restored peace to the Rio Grande by approaching his counterpart, Lorenzo Cortina, commander of the Tamaulipas militia at Reynosa, to arrange a truce. The two signed an agreement on January 13, 1833, combining their forces into a single unit commanded by Cortina.[125]

The struggle between the concepts of federalism and centralism continued even after the election of Santa Anna as president in April, 1833. Elected as a liberal reformer, the new executive left the office in charge of his vice-president, Valentín Gómez Farías, and retired to his plantation in June to await political developments. A true liberal Federalist, Farías instituted a number of reforms directed against the privileges of the military and the church, and before the end of 1833 the offended elements united to recover their former power. Approached by conservative agents, the wily president, aware where real political power lay, returned to office in April, 1834, and began reversing the changes made during his absence.

[125] Convention, January 13, 1833, in *Restorer of Tamaulipas*, January 18, 1833, Matamoros Archives, Barker History Center, University of Texas at Austin.

Between 1834 and 1835, gradually strengthening his position with the support of the army and the church, Santa Anna dissolved Congress, the state legislatures, and even certain *ayuntamientos* that opposed his dictatorship.

During the period of reform Bradburn retired from active service and lived quietly near Matamoros with his wife and son, Andrés. Now past his forty-sixth year, the general raised vegetables for the Matamoros market on his farm along the river road below town. A Texas visitor noted that he had the respect of the foreign community in the city, even the Anglo merchants. His former colleague, George Fisher, also lived in Matamoros, where he maintained a bookstore and stationery shop and served as an English translator and land agent. Fisher had expected to return to Galveston as customs collector early in 1833, but the administration was unable to provide the necessary troops to enforce the laws. Instead Fisher secured a position as commissary for war under General Vicente Filisola, who succeeded Mier y Terán, but his political enemies forced his dismissal before the end of 1833. In retaliation Fisher published the *Mercurio de Matamoros*, a newspaper opposed to Santa Anna, which he edited until September, 1835, when supporters of the dictator ordered him to leave. Fisher returned to New Orleans, where he joined forces with other refugees plotting the downfall of Santa Anna.[126]

[126] J. H. Kuykendall, "Sketches of Early Texians," p. 46, transcript, James Hampton Kuykendall Papers, Barker History Center; Mary Fisher Parmenter et al., *The Life of George Fisher (1795–1873) and the History of the Fisher Family in Mississippi*, p. 41.

In 1835 a number of revolts occurred in northeastern Mexico, and the dictator sent his inept brother-in-law, General Martín Perfecto de Cós, to command the Eastern Interior States. In October the Anglo-Texans fired on Centralist Troops at Gonzales and in December laid siege to Cós in Béxar, forcing his surrender. Irritated by the affront to his family and the challenge to his administration, Santa Anna started north to lead the army into Texas in person to punish the Texans and expel the foreigners.

Bradburn at first hesitated to accept a command that would send him back to Texas but finally agreed to serve under General José Urrea, evidently with an understanding that he would not participate in any engagements in eastern Texas. Urrea started his army north along the coast on February 17, heading toward the Nueces River to intercept a force of Anglos who planned to loot the Matamoros customhouse. The leader of the intended raid was Frank W. Johnson, Bradburn's former antagonist at Anahuac. Urrea's advance units routed the filibusterers, though Johnson escaped, and the force continued toward Goliad, where James W. Fannin commanded a group of volunteers from the United States.[127]

Bradburn remained on the lower coast at Copano, the port on the bay of the same name, an arm of Aransas Bay, just north of the Nueces River. Urrea named him commander of the tiny port, the traditional landing for goods destined for San Antonio, to

<hr />

[127] José Urrea, *Diario de las operaciones militares de la division que al mando del general José Urrea*, in Carlos E. Castañeda, ed., *The Mexican Side of the Texas Revolution*, pp. 219–24.

receive expected supplies from Matamoros and defend the bay from attack.

Bradburn therefore missed the action about fifty miles northeast on March 19 and 20, when Urrea's cavalry captured Fannin on the prairie near Coleto Creek. By Santa Anna's order most of the prisoners were executed one week later, in spite of protests by Urrea and others.[128] This massacre, coupled with that at the Alamo on March 6, inspired a spirit of revenge among the Texans, who managed to defeat Santa Anna on April 21 near the San Jacinto River at a site only a few miles west of Anahuac. The Texans captured the dictator the next day and forced him to order Urrea, Filisola, and the other commanders west of the Brazos to return to the interior "beyond the Rio Grande." Had the order been to retreat beyond the Nueces River, the Centralist troops would have been removed beyond the border of Texas, but the Nueces, the southern boundary of Texas, was not well defined, and so the border was unilaterally stretched south to cut through both Tamaulipas and Coahuila.

At Copano on May 12, Bradburn received orders from Filisola, who had been named commander of the retreating Mexican army, to remain at the port and intercept any supply vessels that might arrive there and turn them back to Matamoros. Two schooners were in port, the *Bravo* and the *Segundo Correo*. Bradburn ordered the *Bravo* to take him to the outer island along the Gulf, where he could wait for the long-expected supply ship *Watchman*. After several

[128] Ibid., pp. 241–45.

[121]

days Bradburn returned to Copano, where he received new instructions to send away the vessels in port and retire inland about fifteen miles to Refugio with his sixty troops and cannons and turn them over to Filisola. The general allowed Bradburn to keep a small force, and with them he returned to the coast to wait for the *Watchman*. Conflicting orders later reduced the party to three Yucatecan soldiers and two militiamen from a nearby Irish colony. The six sailed out to the sandbar in Bradburn's small boat, the *Andresito*, named for his son. The tiny force could scarcely have been expected to challenge two privateers that entered the bay on May 27 and 30. Feeling abandoned, Bradburn finally ordered the men to move the boat south through the shallow bays, but when the party landed for the night, two of the soldiers deserted, and the other three became ill. Unable to handle the little craft by himself, Bradburn left it and started on foot down the length of Padre Island. After three days he found a horse and a guide, and on June 13 he finally reached Matamoros, exhausted and ill from exposure.[129]

Bradburn again returned to civilian life, but the Federalist War that began in 1838 thrust him back in the army. The Centralists abandoned Santa Anna in 1836 and again made Bustamante president. The civil war recommenced along the Rio Grande, and Federalists enlisted the aid of volunteers from the new Republic of Texas, which had been created in 1836. Centralist command devolved on Pedro de Am-

---

[129] Filísola to Bradburn, May 25, 1836, in ibid., pp. 267–68.

pudia in July, 1840, but Bradburn and two other generals, Adrian Woll and Nicolás Condelle, refused to serve under him and set off for Mexico City. Without access to military records it is difficult to trace Bradburn's career at this point. By the end of 1840 he had returned to Matamoros, where it was rumored that he had been assigned to help General Rafael Vásquez move against San Patricio, near the Nueces River.[130] Whether or not he did so remains unclear, but he was not with Vásquez in March, 1842, when the latter attacked San Antonio.

The fifty-five-year-old Bradburn became ill mid-April, 1842. He made his will and about a week later, on April 20, he died. He was buried on his ranch. He had bought the property only three months before, though he may have lived there for a number of years. The 4,606-acre tract, known as Puertas Verdes, was one of the land grants issued by Spain in 1794. It stretched less than one mile along the northeastern bank of the Rio Grande but extended a little over seven miles north of the river in Hidalgo County. The exceedingly long, narrow tract was one of many similar ones shaped by the need of each Spanish colonist to front on a body of water. The site of the ranch house and Bradburn's unmarked grave are probably just east of present-day Mission.

Bradburn's widow and his son, who was still a minor in 1842, left for Mexico City soon after his death. Señora Bradburn appointed an attorney to sell the property. The sale was completed by January of

[130] Joseph Milton Nance, *After San Jacinto: The Texas-Mexican Frontier, 1836–1841*, pp. 331, 338.

[123]

the following year. She reserved the burial site from the sale, perhaps intending eventually to be interred alongside her husband. In 1861 the property passed to the Oblate Fathers, who established La Lomita Seminary there. The seminary has no record of Bradburn's grave within the compound.[131]

What happened to the widow remains unclear. Bradburn's son, Andrés Davis Bradburn y Hurtado, became a priest, known as Father Davis. In 1880, when he was about sixty, he sold his inheritance, the Hurtado de Mendoza property known as the House of Tiles, which included the Church and Cemetery of San Diego, in Mexico City.[132]

Lacking descendants concerned about preserving his name and reputation in Texas, Bradburn became the scapegoat for nineteenth-century Texas historians describing the events at Anahuac as the opening salvo in the struggle for independence from Mexico. That Bradburn was obeying orders from his superiors to enforce national laws and was not acting in a capricious or arbitrary manner was ignored by those reveling in the glorious victory of 1836. Most Anglo-Texans preferred their version of history and viewed the Mexican authorities in the same light that their ancestors had viewed England and George III. Their narrow, chauvinistic interpretation prevailed, though at least two of Bradburn's contemporaries, John A.

[131] Abstract of Porción 57, Hidalgo County, Texas, Deed Record A, pp. 265–76; Acto of Possession, Visita General, p. 288, Spanish Archives, General Land Office of Texas, translated copy in Wallisville Heritage Park Archives.

[132] Zamora Plowes, Quince Unas, pp. 304–305.

Williams, of Atascosito, and Samuel May Williams (no relation) understood the colonel's position. Sam Williams set out from San Felipe with volunteers to relieve Bradburn in June, 1832. When he met Piedras returning to Nacogdoches and was told that the pro-government unit was no longer needed, he returned to the Brazos. For his pains in supporting the national government, Williams was labeled a Tory and hanged in effigy.[133] After the fall of the Alamo in 1836, Texans remembered Bradburn as the tyrant who had unjustly jailed the martyred Travis four years earlier, and for a century that fact alone was enough to maintain the colonel's infamous reputation. The Texas press was surprisingly neutral when it announced Bradburn's death, perhaps following the tradition of not speaking disparagingly of the dead. On June 22, 1842, two months after he died, the *Houston Telegraph and Texas Register* carried this notice: "Gen. Bradburn, who had long been in the Mexican service, and formerly commanded the garrison of Anahuac, lately died at Matamoros."

Revisionist historians, insulated from the past by a comfortable number of years, can look again at events in Texas and, aided by additional primary materials, come to less prejudicial appraisals of controversial men like Bradburn. It is evident that he was not the "unprincipled renegade" painted by Foote. He was obviously a competent, courageous, and trustworthy military commander, or he would not have held leadership positions between 1815 and 1818 for

---

[133] Margaret Swett Henson, *Samuel May Williams: Early Texas Entrepreneur*, pp. 41–42; "Bradburn Memorial."

which he was chosen by his fellow soldiers. His appointments in the Mexican army rested on privilege, but it seems doubtful that he would have continued to hold responsible positions if he was truly incompetent. He probably was always arrogant—successful military commanders are neither timid nor humble. The mere fact that he was a career officer in the Mexican army caused Anglo-Texans to view his actions in a negative manner. To them he appeared a traitor to his native land when he insisted on enforcing laws that they did not completely understand, laws designed to "Mexicanize" Texas while the Anglo residents were endeavoring to do the opposite.

The Anglo-Texans never understood the difference between the Mexican republic and that of the United States, and they continued to believe that they carried with them into a foreign land all the rights and privileges guaranteed to American citizens by the Constitution of the United States. How could military rule prevail along the coast and international border when the United States had no such restrictions? Anglo-Texans believed that states' rights should take precedence over unpopular national rulings, a sentiment that their contemporaries in South Carolina strongly supported. Opponents of the tariff in Mexican Texas voiced some of the same arguments that the Nullifiers employed in South Carolina. Moreover, when Bradburn arrested Travis and Jack for sedition and mutinous conduct within his military jurisdiction, the Texans could not understand that they had no recourse to bail, indictment, a speedy trial by a jury of one's peers, or any of the other freedoms guaranteed to citizens of the United States. The Mexican Constitution of 1824 provided none of those rights and only grudgingly granted minuscule freedom of speech and press. These concepts, descending from English common law, were foreign to Spanish law, a fact apparently not understood even by Anglo-Texan lawyers, most of whom had yet to learn enough Spanish to read the laws of their new country.

As a military commander Bradburn acted correctly in his arrest of Travis and Jack, and neither their imprisonment nor the plan to send them to Matamoros for a hearing was cruel or "absolute tyranny," as contemporaries charged. Emotionalism, frustration, and uncertainty about the arrests caused the Texans to resort to such hyperbole in describing Bradburn's action. Nor did the colonel arrest the men because of wounded vanity, as Eugene C. Barker says in his biography of Austin. A bogus letter purportedly from Bradburn's friend describing an advancing filibustering army is scarcely an innocent practical joke, especially at a time when the New Orleans newspapers were publishing letters urging an invasion of Texas.

As for the charges leveled against Bradburn that he was instrumental in closing the new *ayuntamiento* at Liberty, it is clear from the date of Father Muldoon's letter to Austin that General Mier y Terán, before he left on November 24, 1831, had ordered the reduction of the Atascosito community as the seat of government and the installation of the court at Anahuac. Because both Liberty and Anahuac were within the coastal reserve forbidden to foreigners, the order creating the *ayuntamiento* was within the power of the commandant general and was not solely a prerogative of Madero as state land commissioner.

Bradburn's final offense in the eyes of the Anglo-Texans was his refusal to join Santa Anna's reform movement with them. He, of course, never contemplated such a step because his career was with the established government. By 1832, Bradburn was a rigid conservative Centralist and unlikely to be attracted to any reform movement afoot. He was acquainted with his immediate superiors, and if his Texas campaign had gone well, he would have expected to be promoted. His loyalty to the established government made him the enemy of his former countrymen once they had decided to utilize the civil war and *santanismo* for their own purposes.

Thus George Fisher and Juan Davis Bradburn, both foreign-born Mexican officials, were unpopular with the Anglo-Texans for their adherence to the Centralist government in 1832. Fisher, ever a political opportunist, redeemed himself in the eyes of the Texans when he joined Federalist refugees in New Orleans in 1835 to promote an invasion of Mexico to oppose Santa Anna. He eventually settled in Houston and was a respected citizen until 1850, when he emigrated to California. Bradburn, however, remained loyal to his adopted country and its conservative party until his death.

APPENDIX 1
Memorial of Colonel Juan Davis Bradburn
concerning the Events at Anahuac, 1831–1832

Because of the importance of what happened in the Department of Texas and the interest that every Mexican
must feel under the circumstances, I feel that it is my duty
to acquaint my superiors and the nation in general of the
many incidents, many of them insignificant at first glance,
which contributed to the loss of those important territo-
ries beginning in 1830 and continuing until June 30,
1832. Some persons who claimed that I behaved as a despot motivated by my own feelings unjustly gave rise to

This account, hand-written in Spanish, was prepared for the commandant general of the Eastern Interior States, Vicente Filisola, by Bradburn in 1832, perhaps in New Orleans or while on his way back to the Rio
Grande. As an apologia for his actions, Bradburn's memorial must be
evaluated just as carefully as those of contemporary Texans, but at least
his was written soon after the attack on Anahuac instead of years later, as
were most of the Anglo-Texan narratives.

This draft is in the Henry R. Wagner Texas and Middle West Collection of the Beinecke Rare Book and Manuscript Library, Yale University, New Haven, Connecticut, Whether a final copy exists in some Mexican archive is unknown, but Filisola used some of the information in his
Memorias para la historia de la guerra de Tejas . . . , published in 1849. The
curator of the Beinecke Library does not know how or when Wagner secured the document. Translations made by Alan Probert and John V. Clay
are deposited at the Beinecke Library and at the Sam Houston Regional
Library and Research Center at Liberty, Texas. This version is a composite
of the two translations modified and edited by me with the approval of the
translators.

complaints against me [although] they result from personal hatred and their own interests, or the force of circumstances.

Early in 1830 I was in Matamoros on leave granted by the Supreme Government when His Excellency Señor don Manuel de Mier y Terán, Commandant General of the Eastern Interior States, arrived. When my leave expired I reported to him and he decided to send me to a locality in his jurisdiction and thereafter, I was under his command. At that period it was intended that Mexican governing bodies should be established among the frontier colonies particularly along the virtually uninhabited Gulf Coast. Galveston Bay attracted the attention of the Government, and Señor Terán decided to send me there to establish a colony which later took the name of Anahuac.

I left the Brazos de Santiago aboard the schooner *Alabama Packet* at the end of October accompanied by Lieutenant Ignacio Domínguez, who came as quartermaster, by Sublieutenant don Juan María Pacho with 13 soldiers from the Company of Pueblo Viejo, and by Señor José Rincón with 20 recruits from the 12th Battalion and 8 convict soldiers, all assigned to found a town on the most favorable portion of Galveston Bay. General Terán issued my instructions which I followed exactly, and which in brief consisted in the establishment of a new community, a village which would be populated largely with native Mexicans, and which would be protected by a fort, [and] charged with carrying into effect the provisions of the Law of April 6, 1830. The said instructions consisting of 19 articles, also ordered me to recognize the petitions of already established settlers in the area so that the Government could issue titles. Above all [the instructions] provided that we deport ourselves in complete harmony with all the colonies, but unfortunately as we will see later on, it was impossible to maintain the friendly relationships so much recommended.

Following a voyage of [6] days, we arrived at a place called Pere [Perry's Point] which was suitably situated to be selected as the site of the community we were going to establish.

A few days after our arrival one civilian, don Francisco Madero, appeared there as a Commissioner of the State of Coahuila y Texas. This gentleman came in compliance with orders like my own from my superior in the General Government. He, like me, was to grant titles, found a community, name civil officials, etc. Never did Señor Madero explain to me the objectives of his commission although I knew that he was undertaking similar responsibilities so like my own, and being convinced that it would be virtually impossible for two Commissioners to perform the same mission, I sent my Adjutant, Domínguez, to politely request a conference with him. But he refused, which led to several very heated communications between us on this subject. However, although complete harmony continued between us, unfavorable rumors spread among the settlers. There were even those who tried to spread the idea that the General Government did not intend to give them the land on which they were settled and that I would not issue titles. The ill feeling reached such a high pitch that the settlers at Atascosito and San Jacinto armed themselves with the intent to attack me in our newly established community of Anahuac, [and] from which they probably would have been able to oust us since we were barely settled. Señor Juan Williams became the leader of the settlers and the uprising would have inevitably occurred had I not sent Lieutenant Pacho with a squad of soldiers to demand an interview to eliminate the basic causes of the revolt. On reaching the ranch of Señor Smith I ordered that Commissioner don Francisco Madero be summoned to the essential interview, at which we both agreed that we would suspend carrying out our commissions until we could consult with our repective superiors. But no sooner had the Commissioner contacted Juan Williams alone than he reneged and asked for time to consider what had to be done. A meeting was set for 9 A.M. the following day, but neither he nor his surveyor, José María Carbajal, appeared, so I considered it advisable to bring them to Anahuac. Carbajal, speaking English, promoted discord and absolute disobedience among the colonists. In

[131]

my opinion, this was the only certain way to insure tranquillity there, and also to protect against an attack on the small military troop under my command. These events resulted in continuing ill feelings towards the General Government by many of the settlers. My conduct in this affair was approved by His Excellency, Señor General don Manuel Mier y Terán and the General Government.

While these upheavals were disturbing our countryside, we laid out our town and began making rapid progress until November, 1831, when Señor Terán came to Anahuac. All the surrounding settlements came to see our new village and its fine location excited rivalry on the part of the inhabitants of Harrisburg and Brazoria. Empresario don Estevan Austin used all of his influence to quiet the feelings of the settlers at San Felipe, but those from Harrisburg viewed with displeasure a federal establishment so close by, and which without doubt would sooner or later stop the smuggling that they practiced along the coast. The residents of Harrisburg sent out the schooner *Champion*, advising the captain to avoid paying me the tonnage due, although doubtless they told him that I might use force to compel obedience, having been commissioned Captain of the Port and acting Administrator of the Customhouse by the General Government.

[With] the impossibility of enforcing the laws against smuggling from Anahuac [which was] 38 leagues distant from Brazoria and the Brazos River, it became necessary to name a commissioner at that port to enforce the Law of April 6, 1830, and also to keep an eye on the arrival of foreigners and slaves. To better decide on the nomination of such a commissioner and to avoid ill feeling among the settlers of San Felipe and Brazoria, I consulted with Señor Samuel Williams (Sr. Austin's agent), requesting him to choose some resident agreeable to the settlers and to him, the choice falling on Juan Austin, who, however, refused the appointment. Later Doctor William Dobie Dunlap, a merchant from Anahuac, was selected, but he met so much opposition that he resigned. Then I sent Captain James Lindsay with a sergeant and 10 soldiers from my small force, but at the same time, don Juan Austin arrived and asked to take the post, which [request] for political reasons was granted although he had scorned the chance earlier. Señor Lindsay remained as Captain of the Port and don Juan Austin as Administrator, which appointments restored obedience and tranquillity. In September, Lieutenant Domínguez went to take Lindsay's place until Señor George Fisher should arrive, he having been designated to fill the post.

No sooner had I notified the communities of Fisher's appointment than I found determined opposition at Brazoria, where the residents refused to accept him, much less obey his orders for ship captains to sail around to Anahuac. This unjust regulation resulted in the ship *Nelson* firing on the soldiers and a force of 50 men who left Brazoria to attack, wounding one. The small force that I had was too small to enforce obedience of the settlers, and Fisher, on the other hand, added to the ill feeling and rebellion by his actions. It reached such a point with the merchants, in particular Señores Morgan and Reid, that I found it necessary to overrule certain orders that I considered improper which brought down on me the hatred of the State Administrator, who thereafter incited those he could influence to oppose me.

November, when Señor Terán arrived at Anahuac, was a time of entire satisfaction for me. I wanted to be relieved of my command of the place although most of the residents and settlers said that they wanted me to stay. Most of my officers, tired from all the responsibilities of founding a new community in the wilderness, felt obliged to complain to His Excellency against me, but he quickly made them see that their objections were unfounded, and he tried to reconcile us. Also, the General overruled as unimportant the complaints against me that emanated from the Departments of Béxar and Saltillo, approving in strong terms my military conduct and recognizing the progress that had been made, due chiefly to all of us having done more than had been hoped. He returned to Matamoros praising the usefulness of the new community to the nation.

Before he left, the General gave me orders to buy the

cannons in Brazoria and either to install them as a battery at the mouth of the Brazos River or take them to Anahuac in order to take them away from the colonists. His Excellency also gave me instructions necessary for the forming of a municipality at Anahuac, since it was then only a military settlement. (I state this to prove to the public that Señor Terán did not intend to name civil authorities at other places than here.) To all of which I have given compliance whenever circumstance permitted.

During the months of December, 1830, and January, 1831, Juan Austin and his associates sent agents to the several colonies to inquire into the feelings relative to making themselves independent of the Mexican Government. They learned that there was still much disagreement about the matter. Several letters of Colonel don Estevan Austin and of Juan Austin on this subject have been sent to the Commandant General from New Orleans and New York. I received from the United States of America several [letters] referring to the preparations of weapons, supplies, and volunteers for that objective. Meanwhile, false rumors circulated through the colonies to incite animosity against me and the Federal responsibilities under my direction. We knew, also, that to carry out their plans, they would have to use the schooners *Nelson*, *William A. Tyson*, *Sabine*, and others, and our suspicions were confirmed when the above schooners sailed out of the Brazos without paying the required duties and firing on the troops that tried to oppose their departures.

These same schooners returned to the Brazos armed with cannon to enter forcibly, [and were] protected by the settlers at Brazoria, who took up arms under the leadership of Juan Austin. At almost the same time in January, a resident of San Felipe de Austin reinforced the certainty that a conspiracy was planned by the residents by bringing to my office an important document containing the names of ten of the principal residents of San Felipe, who held meetings to plot the independence of Texas from the Central Government. This document, together with data on all the events of those months, was sent to the Commandant General.

Since political matters formed one of the principal instructions that I had received from His Excellency, I granted an interview requested by Colonel [Stephen F.] Austin to discuss our differences in a friendly manner and to stop the quarrels that were plaguing the settlements as well as to halt the preparations the settlers were making. It was planned to be held in Harrisburg, but the Administrator, Fisher, who should have participated in the conference, refused to take part and only tried to discredit me with my own superiors because of my willingness to participate, saying that I worked against the Mexicans. But all these slanders and lies vanished because of the official correspondence and private letters which I sent to Señor Terán relating to the interview, and these documents will convince the Government relative to my military conduct during my command at Anahuac.

Quartermaster Juan María Pacho was replaced by Lieutenant don Juan Cortina, and the latter took charge of the construction of the fort but wasted much time making changes in my instructions. Eventually, Marine Lieutenant José María Jiménez was put in charge of the construction work. But when completed, I saw that the redoubt did not dominate the surroundings, nor was it possible to construct a moat, so I ordered the work elevated and built a parapet of beams and stakes. Unfortunately this change, which I made for our greater safety, was not to Lieutenant Jiménez's liking, and he became my enemy from that time on.

About this time, Lieutenant Colonel don Domingo Ugartechea arrived at Galveston with a contingent of troops and orders to build a small fort at the mouth of the Brazos River. He brought with him instructions necessary to his assignment, and like all other military commanders in Texas at that time, he was charged with using political methods before the use of arms. I added to these a list of names of settlers who had become known as leaders of the enemies of the Government, a list which, as we shall see, fell into the hands of those mentioned in spite of the warning I gave Ugartechea about their trustworthiness.

Several important events concerning my safety occurred in Brazoria unknown to me. Juan Austin at the head of 300 men marched against me to demand that some prisoners be handed over to them although they were being interrogated for serious crimes against the Anahuac military establishment. The expedition came, accompanied by Lieutenant Domínguez, who was under Colonel Ugartechea's command, and Juan Austin as the leader, to upset the tranquillity of the town and attack our fort. When the commissioners arrived, we knew that a small body of troops were in the vicinity. I therefore immediately assembled my officers and at once went with Señor Austin and Lieutenant Domínguez to a meeting, ordering Lieutenant Cortina to preside as the senior officer. All of us having heard the reading of the letter from Señor Ugartechea and the claims that Juan Austin made, the Prosecutor took the floor and explained the reasons for the imprisonment of William B. Travis, Patrick Jack, and company with such clarity, quoting the order in the Military Regulations which gives the right to judge in Court Martial the crimes they had committed, that even Austin himself was convinced. He stated with chagrin the reason for their coming and said that he had been duped.

We had just reached agreement over our misunderstandings when Lieutenant Domínguez, who came with the rebels, advised Lieutenant Cortina and the rest of the officers that our horses were stolen. It was not necessary to repeat the statement: all my officers shouted, " . . . to arms, Mexicans . . ." and went voluntarily to their respective posts. Lieutenant Cortina, who until then had not wanted to believe my warnings about what was going to happen, and all the other officers behaved admirably, working on the fort all night without rest, and they were obedient to my orders.

The imprudence of an officer complicated the circumstances. He had acquired a young Anglo girl from an inhabitant of Texas. The Texan was tarred and feathered by the settlers, and feelings ran very high against the garrison. The town of Anahuac was so excited that it was necessary to call out the troops at two o'clock in the morning to stop disorders stemming from this incident. Juan Austin,

Juan Williams, the Alcalde of Anahuac, with another member of the *ayuntamiento* aided in this scandalous attack and soon organized a company of 80 men who joined the rebellious neighbors of Brazoria. They handed me an ultimatum from their officers demanding that I hand over the prisoners, Patrick Jack, James Lindsay, and Monroe Edwards, and added that I should also deliver to them two Mexican convict soldiers who had attempted to rape a woman of the settlement.

These scandalous happenings which took place on the 26th resulted in several reports. Lieutenants Pacho and Silva and Doctor García Ugarte stood firm at the Plaza de Malinche despite the arrival of 13 armed men who stood ready to assault the fort, liberate the prisoners, and kill me. On the night of the 26th, the insurrection was such that at the suggestion of Lieutenant Carlos Ocampo, who was acting chief of the garrison, and Lieutenant Cortina, who was still sick in bed, I ordered my officers to meet to consider whether the prisoners were being punished according to law in order that we might appease the rebels, which was done more for political reasons than for any other.

The rebels having been dispersed, Lieutenant Cortina and the entire garrison went to work anew on the redoubt strongholds and in mounting cannon to prevent any further assault on our flag. Lieutenant Cortina gave an extraordinary example of obedience and perseverance in all this work.

Another most unusual thing which I must mention to explain the entire truth and which I have not been able to understand is how the list of leaders that I had given to Señor Ugartechea happened to fall into the hands of my enemies and made the trouble worse.

One matter which caused me much trouble and brought down the hatred of the community against me was the protection I gave to two escaped slaves. In August, 1831, the slaves appeared and claimed to have come from the United States of the North, begging me to extend to them the protection of the Mexican flag. Since my instructions did not provide for the case, I immediately sent them to the fort to work until I could consult with the Commandant General of the Eastern States to find out what I should do with them. He decided that my reply to the slaveowners, if they appeared to claim them, [should be] that military commanders had no authority at the frontier to decide national matters and that the claimants could register their complaints to the Government through the American Minister in Mexico [City] so that a precedent could be established to decide similar cases. Señor don Manuel Mier y Terán, who by good luck happened to be in Anahuac when the [owner's] agents came to claim the slaves, told them what he had ordered me to do in his letter. I have scrupulously followed his orders relative to this matter despite my having realized that it could cause me a thousand important problems. I knew at the time that powerful groups were forming to demand that I hand over those slaves. Some enemies of the Government and the settlers in general blamed me for these decisions and had made much of this pretext to rise in arms against the garrison at Anahuac.

Another excuse used by the colonists against me stemmed from the loss of the schooner *Topaz*, but in this matter my reports place me beyond responsibility. After the events which took place aboard the schooner *Topaz* between Matamoros and Anahuac, Marine Lieutenant don José María Jiménez, to whom I had given command [of the vessel] after his arrival in Galveston, refused to follow my orders. After having inventoried the cargo of the vessel, he ordered it delivered to the warehouse of the deceased Captain Rider, the owner. Unfortunately the vessel was lost at the mouth of the Brazos River, as may be found in the depositions regarding the events aboard which are in the files of the Commandant General. It is desirable that the whole account of this affair be placed before the public, [and] even the revolution and the death of Señor Terán should not stop the course of this affair, nor leave unpunished crimes of this magnitude. This matter has not failed to irritate the feelings of the settlers, and furthermore, they could bring up questions between the two governments since it is well known how many untruthful things have been published in the papers of North America accusing Mexican officers who were aboard the *Topaz* of being criminals, calling them thieves and murderers, when there could not have been anthing else aboard an unloaded schooner which they themselves chartered for transportation. During the first days that the insurgents spent in Anahuac, the schooner *Marta*, [which] I had sent to Matamoros for funds and supplies for the garrison, anchored in Galveston Bay. Lieutenant Colonel Félix María Subarán and Sergeant Campo were on board, imprisoned for political opinions and being sent to Fort Terán to be put under the orders of Colonel José de las Piedras. Having disembarked and being short of men, particularly officers, I appointed him [Subarán] as deputy commander, persuaded that every Mexican loves his country when it is threatened by foreign enemies, and I was not wrong. Subarán behaved very well in every commission that I assigned to him, and he continued in this service until July 1, when Señor Colonel don José de las Piedras arrived.

Piedras came as a result of my letter begging men and ammunition for war, and in a few days he marched and arrived at the village of the Coushatta Indians. As he neared Anahuac, he encountered resistance on the part of the settlers. He made a peace treaty with them, offering to relieve me of command. I agreed to it all since General Terán had told me that I could not expect aid in men or money because of the revolution in the interior. A Council of War was held in the quarters of Señor don José de las Piedras which considered the political events of the day and our local situation. I made the statement that the revolution in Texas was based wholly on pretexts, but if relieving me of command would reestablish peace and order, I would be willing to yield in everything with the proviso that under no circumstance would I be given the same command again, since this move would make the settlers believe that I had been punished. Before the arrival of Colonel Piedras it was said that I was jailed in Anahuac on his orders.

The Council again conferred command on me, although Lieutenant Colonel Subarán expected it, as some official had promised it to him. But recognizing my precarious situation, I handed over the command of the garrison and fort to Colonel Piedras, convinced that destruction of the federal establishment was inevitable and despite knowing that from the moment when I surrendered my command my own life would be in danger in the midst of the colonists. On July 2, I effected the change of command to Colonel Piedras as commander of Anahuac, and he immediately released the prisoners, Travis, Jack, and company, as well as the sailors from the schooner *Topaz* and others no less criminal. He sent them to the village of Liberty in charge of the Alcalde there, and I at the same time delivered to him [Piedras] certain documents so that he would be fully aware of reasons for their imprisonment and would have information for following up their trials, which resulted in him writing me a letter asking me to again take command, to which I answered that my departure was urgent because of the perils to which I was now exposed.

Lieutenant Cortina was therefore named commander of Anahuac, and Colonel Piedras left to return to Nacogdoches, leaving orders that Lieutenant Colonel Subarán should follow soon afterwards in spite of my warning him of the dangerous consequences which could break out as a result. He did not want to take part in anything, although at 3 o'clock in the morning some of the officers came to my house to tell me that the garrison was disgusted, particularly with the newly named commander. I sent word of what was happening to Colonel Piedras, who told me to have no fear about it, but at the moment of departing, he gave me a letter advising that [while] Señor Cortina had been nominated, [Piedras] requested me to take command in case of a new attack.

Since Señor Subarán's arrival, two new redoubts had been constructed without delaying the building of the warehouses; thus, the stronghold was now able to dominate the Plaza de Malinche. This last redoubt, which the officers called Fort Davis, was designed by Lieutenant Colonel Subarán and me. It was located above the edge of the Battery Plaza, with the water at its base, a moat and a drawbridge, and a barracks inside, all of heavy construction and equipped to handle 50 men. I put a 6 caliber cannon of my own ready for mounting during any invasion. This redoubt allowed the resumption of commerce, and the stronghold's flanks were defended by land and water, with the field between the two fortifications free and safe for the horses of the garrison. We were still preparing ourselves for defense on the 3rd day after Colonel Piedras had left Anahuac. At this moment Señor Añorga notified me that his commander, Señor Cortina, ordered him to let me know that the soldiers had disobeyed him and had assembled in the plaza in rebellion. Having heard the same from Subarán, I called the officers together in Lieutenant Cortina's quarters. They wanted me to resume command, but having wished to be sure of the intention of the troops and that their declaration was in favor of Señor Santa Anna, I asked Lieutenant Colonel [Subarán] as his immediate superior, and I immediately gave orders that he be recognized, hoping that this measure would restore peace and good sense, which we so badly needed to resist our common enemies.

Unfortunately, at the moment the mutiny began, Travis, Jack, and company, who Señor Piedras had sent to the town of Liberty, came back and, buying some barrels of aguardiente, invited the soldiers to their houses to thus seduce them from their duty to their officers. In these circumstances, [Travis] succeeded in involving Señor Subarán, who became drunk and foolish.

On July 2nd [12th] it was necessary to assemble the troops and place them in readiness for marching without the knowledge of the commander [Subarán]. But seeing the disorder and being unable to correct it, I begged Cortina as Administrator of the Customhouse to use all of his influence to charter two vessels to transport the garrison to Matamoros, convinced that if we marched overland, we would lose many men due to the inevitable lack of money and food.

From the moment I surrendered the command, my

life was continuously in danger despite there being a guard at my door. At night my enemies, directed by Travis, who now had control of Anahuac, would sneak up to my quarters, which made me decide to leave. I told my intentions to Señor Subarán, and that officer agreed to everything so long as I went by water, and for that reason he had a boat delivered to me on the pretext that I was going to a ranch. The rebels blockaded my departure with two larger boats than mine and kept up a continuous watch across the bay, which forced me to go by land. My friends provided guides and horses, risking their own lives so that I might go safely. The 13th of July Lieutenants Ocampo, Cortina, and Montero also fled with Sublieutenant Domínguez, Cadet Añorga, and Lieutenant Miguel Nieto with all the cavalry. On the same day that all this group had abandoned the fort, I left Anhuac at 8 P.M. Having gone near the house of my guide, I learned that the officers mentioned were in his house. I asked for an interview with Lieutenant Cortina, who told me the reason for their departure, because despite [my] having left after they did, I did not know what had happened. [Cortina] told me that he had asked the Alcalde of Atascosito for help to continue me in my post [and] the alcalde undertook to gather the men. But some of them found the arrangement distasteful as I had outlined it, claiming that the fort was not easy to take when defended by cannon. Cortina volunteered to take it himself with 20 men, and to make this possible, a messenger was ordered to go to the Sabine to bring back the men assembled there.

Without being well informed of what happened, later I learned that Colonel José Antonio Mexía had arrived at Galveston Bay, [and] Lieutenant Colonel Subarán went on board the vessels with his troops, cannon, and ammunition. This took place after I had already gone to Louisiana. After the departure of the Lieutenant Colonel, Lieutenant don Juan Cortina, Lieutenant Manuel Montero, and Cadet Añorga were the only ones of the garrison who stayed in Anahuac, having to suffer the insults from the settlers.

In the course of my travels, which I performed incognito, from Anahuac to the banks of the Mississippi, I came across many people I had known in the settlements and I asked them where they were going so far away. They answered to help our brothers drive the Spaniards out of Texas. Traveling in this way, I learned the opinions and hopes of the principal inhabitants of the whole countryside. One judge who lives on the banks of the Río Matan [said] he could easily have enlisted 4,000 men for the Texas campaign. It is a very popular topic among the people of that State and of the United States of the North, and from what I already know from the time that I spent in command in Texas, it is necessary to have a sizable force to reduce the settlers and the inhabitants of the said district to obedience to Mexican laws because until now they have only observed Anglo-American laws.

The settlements that now exist between the River Neches and the Sabine may be estimated at 2,000 or more inhabitants at least, and many of them have large and important ranches, some with 40 or more slaves. Cotton, corn, and wheat are the principal crops; these settlers raise cattle in great numbers and are able to export their products via the Neches River and also to import from New Orleans all that they need for their ranches.

Finally I will comment to the Supreme Government that lawyers Samuel Williams, Jefferson Chambers, Ira R. Lewis, and Abner Kuykendall raised a company of 80 or 100 volunteers and they were ready to defend Anahuac. But they abandoned their plans when they met Señor Piedras with his treaties of peace, which he had just signed with the insurgent settlers. But the revolution having continued its spread throughout Texas because of the circumstances, the rebellious settlers burned in effigy the first three leaders who were coming to my assistance, but they did not do the same to Father Michael Muldoon only because it was too costly to provide a priest's garment. With this increase in strength I could have defended myself much better if they had arrived in time since in Anahuac I could depend on one other company because all the settlers who lived near Atascosito were always sympathetic to the Mexicans. Some of them have had to claim neutrality, or even to have taken the other side, in order to save their own lives and belongings from the rebels.

All of this I place before the Señor Commandant General of the Eastern Interior States so that when the time and opportunity come to punish the settlers, he will take into account those who have been involved by their own free will and those who were forced into it.

Also I should point out to every officer who may take command of the troops in Texas that the scarcity of money has always been and always will be the cause of insubordination of the troops. Otherwise all of their orders will be useless, because it has been necessary to live on borrowed money loaned by the enemy. Nothing has caused so much trouble in Anahuac as when the schooner *Marta*, which I had sent to Matamoros for the payroll and provisions, came back without a cent. Food and the small loans which they advanced to us at Anahuac to eke out our misery were paid after much delay by a commissary that had no funds. The officers found themselves obliged to sell their scrip for from 5 to 50 percent discount, and the soldiers, having received only half of their wages, were far in debt and annoyed with the military service at that place [Anahuac].

On my departure from Anahuac, the population was about 1,000 inhabitants and on my arrival in New Orleans where I stayed one month, I gave an account of my experiences in the Texas colonies to the Mexican consul.

Appendix 2
Article 26 of the Military laws Governing Anahuac under Which Bradburn Arrested Travis, Jack, and the Others in May–June, 1832

Sedición.

Art. 26 Los que emprendieren cualquiera sedición, conspiración ó motín, ó indujeren a cometer estos delitos contra mi real servicio, seguridad de las plazas y paises de mis dominios, contra la tropa, su comandante ú oficiales, serán ahorcados en cualquiera número que sean, y los que hubieren tenido noticia, y no lo delaten luego que puedan, sufrirán la misma pena.

Sedition

Art. 26 Those who engage in sedition, conspiracy, or mutiny, or induce others to commit these crimes against my royal service, against the security of the town and countryside of my dominions, against the troops, their commandant of officers, shall be hanged, whatever the number may be, and those who have been warned and do not leave, can suffer the same penalty.

SOURCE: Ministerio de Guerra y Marina, *Ordenanza militar para el régimen, disciplina, subordinación y servicio del ejército*, 2:230. The article was obviously adapted in 1833 from previous Spanish military codes.

Bibliography

PRIMARY SOURCES

Manuscript Collections
Private Papers

Everett B. Graff Collection. Newberry Library. Chicago.
Juan E. Hernández y Dávalos Collection. Benson Latin American Library. University of Texas at Austin.
James Hampton Kuykendall Papers. Barker History Center. University of Texas at Austin.
Nicholas Labadie Papers. Rosenberg Library. Galveston.
Henry R. Wagner Texas and Middle West Collection. Beinecke Rare Book and Manuscript Library. Yale University. New Haven, Connecticut.
Samuel May Williams Papers. Rosenberg Library. Galveston.

Public Documents

Archivo General de las Indias. Seville. Dunn Transcripts. 1763–1818, 1800–19. Barker History Center. University of Texas at Austin.
Archivo General de la Nación. Mexico City. Transcripts. Barker History Center. University of Texas at Austin.
Béxar Archives. Microfilm. Barker History Center. University of Texas at Austin.
Christian County. Kentucky, Tax Roll, 1814.
Matamoros, Tamaulipas Archives. Barker History Center. University of Texas at Austin.
Nacogdoches and Béxar Archives. Translations and other materials. Transcripts. 93 vols. Typescript. Robert Bruce Blake Re-

search Collection. Texas History Center. Houston Public Library. Houston.

Spanish Archives. General Land Office of Texas.

United States Census: Christian County, Kentucky, 1810. Iberville Parish, Louisiana, 1850.

United States Compiled Military Service Records. Records of the Adjutant General, 1780–1917. Record Group 94, War of 1812. National Archives, Washington, D.C.

Published Correspondence

Barker, Eugene C., ed. *The Austin Papers.* Vol. 2. American Historical Association *Annual Report.* 1922. Washington, D.C.: Government Printing Office, 1928.

Gulick, Charles Adams, Jr., et al., eds. *The Papers of Mirabeau Buonaparte Lamar.* 6 vols. Austin: Von Boeckmann-Jones Co., 1921–27.

McLean, Malcolm D., comp. and ed. *Papers Concerning Robertson's Colony in Texas.* 6 vols. Fort Worth: Texas Christian University Press; Arlington: University of Texas at Arlington Press, 1974–79.

Published Memoirs

Anonymous [William Fiske? Ashael Langworthy?]. *A Visit to Texas in 1831.* Houston: Cordovan Press, 1975.

Filisola, Vicente. *Memorias para la historia de la guerra de Tejas.* . . . 2 vols. Mexico City: R. Rafael, 1848–49.

Johnson, Frank W. "Further Account . . . of the First Breaking Out of Hostilities." *The Texas Almanac for 1859.* In *The Texas Almanac, 1857–1873: A Compendium of Texas History.* Comp. James Day. Waco: Texian Press, 1967.

Labadie, Nicholas D. "Narrative of the Anahuac, or Opening Campaign of the Texas Revolution." *The Texas Almanac for 1859* in *The Texas Almanac, 1857–1873: A Compendium of Texas History.* Comp. James Day. Waco: Texian Press, 1967.

Linn, John Joseph. *Reminiscences of 50 Years in Texas.* New York: D. J. Sadler & Co., 1883.

Pearson, P. E., ed. "Reminiscences of Judge Edwin Waller." *Quarterly of the Texas State Historical Association* 4 (July, 1900): 33–53.

Robinson, William Davis. *Memoirs of the Mexican Revolution.* Philadelphia: Privately printed, 1820.

Scates, William B. "Early History of Anahuac." *The Texas Almanac for 1873*. In *The Texas Almanac, 1857–1873: A Compendium of Texas History*. Comp. James Day. Waco: Texian Press, 1967.

Urrea, José. *Diario de las operaciones militares de la división que al mando del General José Urrea*. . . . Victoria, Durango: Privately printed, 1838. In Carlos E. Castañeda, ed. *The Mexican Side of the Texas Revolution*. Austin: Graphic Ideas, 1970.

Published Documents

Gammel, Hans P. N., comp. *The Laws of Texas, 1822–1897*. 10 vols. Austin: Gammel Book Co., 1898.

Ministerio de Guerra y Marina de Mexico. *Ordenanza militar para el régimen, disciplina, subordinación y servicio del ejército*. Vol. 2. Mexico City: Imprenta de Galván, 1833.

Newspapers

La Águila méjicana (Matamoros), 1828. Translated typescript of article in Wallisville Heritage Park Archives, Wallisville, Texas.

Galveston News, 1845.

Houston Telegraph and Texas Register, 1842.

Louisiana Advertiser (New Orleans), 1832.

Mexican Citizen (San Felipe), 1831.

New Orleans Bee, 1832.

New Orleans Courier, 1832.

Niles' Weekly Register (Baltimore), 1815.

Texas Gazette (San Felipe), 1830–32.

Texas National Register (Washington-on-the-Brazos), 1845.

SECONDARY SOURCES

Books

Alamán, Lucas. *Historia de Méjico desde . . . el año de 1808 hasta la época presente*. 5 vols. Mexico City: Editorial Jus, 1942.

Alessio Robles, Vito. *Coahuila y Texas desde la consumación de la independencia . . .* 2 vols. Mexico City. Imprenta Universitaria Talleres Gráficos de la Nación, 1946.

Atienza, Julio de. *Títulos nobiliarios hispano americanos*. Madrid: M. Aguilar, 1947.

Bancroft, Hubert Howe. *History of the Mexican People*. New York: Bancroft Co., 1914.

———. *The History of Mexico, 1804–1824.* 6 vols. San Francisco: A. L. Bancroft & Co., 1883–85.

———. *History of the North American States and Texas.* 2 vols. San Francisco: A. L. Bancroft & Co., 1889.

Barker, Eugene C. *The Life of Stephen F. Austin: Founder of Texas, 1793–1836.* Austin: Texas State Historical Association, 1949.

Brown, John Henry. *History of Texas from 1685 to 1892.* . . . 2 vols. Saint Louis, Mo.: L. E. Daniell, 1892.

Carter, James David. *Masonry in Texas: Background, History, and Influence to 1846.* Waco: Committee on Masonic Education and Service, 1955.

Caruso, John Anthony. *The Liberators of Mexico.* Gloucester, Mass.: Peter Smith, 1969.

Casey, Powell A. *Louisiana in the War of 1812.* Baton Rouge, La.: Privately printed, 1963.

Conner, Seymour V. *Texas: A History.* New York: Thomas Y. Crowell Co., 1971.

Diccionario Porrúa, 4th ed. Mexico City: Editorial Porrúa, S.A., 1976.

Fehrenbach, T. R. *Fire and Blood: A History of Mexico.* New York: Macmillan Co., 1973.

———. *Lone Star: A History of Texas and Texans.* New York: Macmillan Co., 1968.

Fernández de Recas, Guillermo S. *Mayorazgos de la Nueva España.* Biblioteca Nacional de México Instituto Bibliográfico Mexicano Publicaciones, no. 10. Mexico City, 1965.

Foote, Henry Stuart. *Texas and the Texans; or, Advance of the Anglo-Americans to the South-West.* 2 vols. Philadelphia: Thomas, Cowperth, Wait & Co., 1841.

Garrett, Jill Knight. *Maury County, Tennessee, Newspaper Abstracts, 1810–1844.* Columbia, Tenn.: Privately printed, 1965.

———. *Maury County Cousins.* Vol. 2. Columbia, Tenn.: Maury County Historical Society, 1971.

Hayes, Charles W. *Galveston: History of the Island and the City.* 2 vols. Austin, Texas: Jenkins Garrett Press, 1974.

Henson, Margaret Swett. *Samuel May Williams: Early Texas Entrepreneur.* College Station: Texas A&M University Press, 1976.

Holley, Mary Austin. *Texas.* Lexington, Ky.: J. Clarke & Co., 1836.

Kennedy, William. *Texas: The Rise, Progress, and Prospects of the Republic of Texas,* 2 vols. London: R. Hastings, 1841.

Louisiana Newspapers, 1794–1961: A Union List. Baton Rouge:

Louisiana Library Association and Louisiana State University Library, 1965.

McDonald, Archie P. *Travis*. Austin: Pemberton Press, 1976.

Mestre Ghigliazza, Manuel, comp. *Efemérides biográficas*. Mexico: J. Porrúa e hijos, 1945.

Miquel i Vergés, José María. *Diccionario de insurgentes*. Mexico City: Editorial Porrúa, S.A., 1969.

Morphis, J. M. *History of Texas from Its Discovery and Settlement.* . . . New York: United States Publishing Co., 1875.

Nance, Joseph Milton. *After San Jacinto: The Texas-Mexican Frontier, 1836–1841*. Austin: University of Texas Press, 1963.

Parmenter, Mary Fisher, et al. *The Life of George Fisher (1795–1873) and the History of the Fisher Family in Mississippi*. Jacksonville, Fla.: H. and W. D. Drew Co., 1959.

Partlow, Miriam. *Liberty, Liberty County, and Atascosito District*. Austin: Pemberton Press, 1974.

Pearson, Jim B., Ben Procter, et al. *Texas: The Land and the People*. Dallas: Hendrick-Long Publishing Co., 1978.

Pierson, Marion John Bennett, comp. *Louisiana Soldiers in War of 1812*. Baton Rouge, La.: Louisiana Genealogical and Historical Society, 1963.

Richardson, Rupert N., et al. *Texas: The Lone Star State*, 3d ed. Englewood Cliffs, N.J.: Prentice-Hall, 1970.

Rivera Cambas, Manuel. *México pintoresco, artístico & monumental*. 3 vols. Mexico: Imprenta de la Reforma, 1880–83.

Robertson, William Spence. *Iturbide of Mexico*. New York: Greenwood Press, 1968.

Taylor, Virginia H. *The Spanish Archives of the General Land Office of Texas*. Austin: Lone Star Press, 1955.

Thrall, Homer S. *A History of Texas*. New York: University Publishing Company, 1885.

———. *A Pictorial History of Texas from the Earliest Visits of European Adventurers to A.D. 1879*. St. Louis: N. D. Thompson & Co., 1879.

Warren, Harris Gaylord. *The Sword Was Their Passport: A History of American Filibustering in the Mexican Revolution*. Baton Rouge: Louisiana State University Press, 1943.

Webb, Walter Prescott, et al., eds. *The Handbook of Texas*. 3 vols. Austin: Texas State Historical Association, 1952, 1976.

Work Projects Administration. *Ship Registers and Enrollments of New Orleans, Louisiana*. 4 vols. Baton Rouge: Louisiana State University Press, 1941.

Yoakum, Henderson. *History of Texas from Its First Settlement in 1685 to Its Annexation to the United States in 1846.* 2 vols. New York: J. S. Redfield, 1855.

Zamora Plowes, Leopoldo. *Quince Uñas y Casanova adventureros.* Mexico City: Talleres Gráficos de la Nación, 1945.

Articles

Devereaux, Linda Ericson. "The Gutierrez-Magee Expedition." *Texana* 11 (1973):52–73.

McLane, William. "William McLane's Narrative of the Magee-Gutierrez Expedition, 1812–1813." Ed. Henry P. Walker. *Southwestern Historical Quarterly* 66 (October, 1962–April, 1963):234–52, 437–79, 569–88.

Morton, Ohland. "Life of General Don Manuel de Mier y Terán as It Affected Texas–Mexican Relations," *Southwestern Historical Quarterly* 46 (July, 1942–April, 1943):22–46, 239–54; 47 (July–October, 1943–January, 1944):29–47, 120–42, 256–67; 48 (July–October 1944):193–218.

Rowe, Edna. "The Disturbance at Anahuac in 1832." *Quarterly of the Texas State Historical Association* 6 (April, 1903):265–94.

Sinks, Julia. "Editors and Newspapers of Fayette County." *Quarterly of the Texas State Historical Association* 1 (July, 1897): 34–47.

Warren, Harris Gaylord. "The Origin of General Mina's Invasion of Mexico." *Southwestern Historical Quarterly* 42 (July, 1938): 3–20.

Unpublished monographs

Graff, Leroy. "The Economic History of the Lower Rio Grande Valley, 1820–1875." Ph.D. dissertation, Harvard University, 1942. Microfilm copy, City College Library, Brownsville, Texas. Photocopy of relevant pages provided by City College Library to John V. Clay, Wallisville Heritage Park Archives.

Letts, Bessie Lucille. "George Fisher." Master's thesis, University of Texas, 1928.

Index